HORSE RACING
IN BERKSHIRE

HORSE RACING IN BERKSHIRE

JAMES DOUGLAS-HOME

ALAN SUTTON

First published in the United Kingdom in 1992
Alan Sutton Publishing Ltd • Phoenix Mill • Far Thrupp
Stroud • Gloucestershire

First published in the United States of America in 1993
Alan Sutton Publishing Inc. • Wolfeboro Falls • NH 03896–9848

British Library Cataloguing in Publication Data

Douglas-Home, James
  Horse Racing in Berkshire
  I. Title
  798.4009422

  ISBN 0-7509-0138-1

Library of Congress Cataloging-in-Publication Data applied for

Typeset in 11/14 Bembo.
Typesetting and origination by
Alan Sutton Publishing Limited.
Printed in Great Britain by
The Bath Press, Avon.

CONTENTS

ACKNOWLEDGEMENTS

Every effort has been made to contact the photographers of the pictures that appear in this book.

The author would like to thank the following for permitting their photographs to be reproduced (roman numerals indicate colour plates):

Molly Baring: p. 31; P. Bertrand: p. 78; Ed Byrne: p. 85; John Crofts: XI; Rex Coleman: p. 38, VII; Gerry Cranham: pp. 46, 68, V; Sheilah Hern: pp. 25, 51, 160; Andy Jessett: p. 127; Trevor Jones: p. 93; Juddmonte Farms: pp. 177, 179; Mirror Group: pp. 40, 41, 106, 126, 159; Minnie Owen: I; Newbury Racecourse Company: pp. 144, 146; Bernard Parkin: VIII, IX, X; Henry Ponsonby: pp. 56, 74, 170, II, III, IV; *Sunday Express*: p. 80; Fiona Vigors: pp. 59, 76, 89, 91, 165; Wallis Photographers: p. 43.

INTRODUCTION

The geographical area which *Horse Racing in Berkshire* covers is that which lies within the current county boundary. The 1974 local government reorganization resulted in a huge chunk of old Berkshire being lost to Oxfordshire. Abingdon, Wantage, Wallingford, the Vale of the White Horse and large sections of what are still known as the Berkshire Downs, the area to the north of the ancient Ridgeway track, are now officially in Oxfordshire.

As a result of these changes, the famous training stables of the Letcombes, East Hendred, Blewbury, Aston Tirrold, Chilton and Wantage, the now defunct Abingdon racecourse, and several thoroughbred studs, of which Aston Upthorpe and Lockinge are notable examples, were moved to Oxfordshire. By the same token, the postal addresses of the famous training establishment at Kingsclere and several studs south of Newbury (Highclere and Gainsborough are examples) would suggest they are in the county of Berkshire. This is not the case. Kingsclere is in fact several miles within the Hampshire border. Highclere and Gainsborough are closer to the county line, but located on the Hampshire side.

Although the 1974 changes deprived Berkshire of some of its racing landmarks, much remains within the present county boundaries. The training villages of Lambourn in the west of the county to Compton further east, which lie in the valleys below the Downs, are where the racehorse is prepared, fed and exercised. The careers of Derby and Grand National winners are shaped and planned from the stables in these Berkshire villages, which include the Queen's own training establishment at West Ilsley.

The county boasts three racecourses. Ascot hosts racing's greatest annual show of pageantry, the four-day June Royal Meeting and perhaps the world's most prestigious race, the King George VI and Queen Elizabeth Stakes, held at the course's July meeting. Newbury was started by the Kingsclere trainer John Porter in 1905 on land between the railway and Greenham Common, and is known as one of the country's premier courses. Little Windsor lies in a crook of the Thames west of the town. Its summer evening fixtures attract vast crowds. Although not attracting the class of horse that her fellow Berkshire courses do, it is one of the country's best attended tracks.

The training yards, their gallops on the downs, the three racecourses and the various studs peppered around the county constitute the broad perspective of this book, which aims to enable the reader to place the various characters, equine and human, in their time and place in Berkshire's racing history, and show what an important part the county has played in the industry's development from its beginnings to the present day.

1
THE BEGINNINGS

Charles II set the seal of royal approval on the sport of horse racing. He converted the Suffolk town of Newmarket into the centre of racing. His court used to adjourn for long periods of the year to Newmarket. The fact that he was prepared to arbitrate in turf disputes and put the force of his patronage behind the sport gave it the necessary impetus to evolve. His racing manager, Tregonwell Frampton, who also served William III, Queen Anne and the first two Georges in the same capacity ensured that Newmarket developed as the focal point of racing during these times.

Although race meetings were held all over the country, Newmarket provided the venue where the top breeders sent their classiest horses to race. The traditional area for horse breeding at this time was Yorkshire. Berkshire and other southern counties were out on a limb as far as racing was concerned.

The somewhat unlikely figure of William, Duke of Cumberland, scourge of the Scots at Culloden, set Berkshire on the racing map. After his military career had come to a premature halt in 1757, after a particularly heavy defeat at the head of the Hanoverian army at Hastenback, George II's son returned to his Windsor home and directed all his energies to building up his stud at Cranbourne Lodge. Although the Duke reputedly had heavy losses on the turf, he succeeded in breeding two horses at his Berkshire stud that were to shape the history of the turf for ever more.

In 1757, Cumberland sent an unraced mare, Cypron, to the stallion, Tartar, who was bred by Edward Leedes in Yorkshire and traced back to one of the original three stallions credited with the formation of the thoroughbred breed, the Byerley Turk. In 1758, Cypron produced a bay colt that Cumberland named Herod. Herod's first outing on the turf was in October 1763, when he beat the Duke of Ancaster's Roman for a purse of 500 gns over Newmarket's Beacon course of 4 miles, 1 furlong and 138 yards. Herod maintained improvement, and in 1764 and 1765 produced two of his best performances when beating the Duke of

Grafton's Antinous in two matches, once again over the Beacon course. When Cumberland died in 1765, Herod was purchased by Sir John Moore and continued to show excellent form. However in August 1766, when running at York, he broke a blood vessel and finished last of the five runners. Although suffering considerably, he recovered and won one of his two races in the spring of 1767, before being retired to Sir John's Neather Hall Stud near Bury St Edmunds in 1768 at a fee of 10 gns.

Herod died in May 1780, having sired the winners of 1,042 races of £201,505, and was the leading sire of winners eight times during his years at stud. Highflyer was Herod's most famous son and with his brothers, Florizel and Woodpecker, did much to perpetuate the Byerley Turk's importance in the development of the thoroughbred breed. But his greatest legacy is the huge incidence of success of his line when mixed with that of the great Eclipse. The names of these two horses are found consistently in the pedigrees of many of the great horses of the late eighteenth and early nineteenth centuries. Herein lies the Duke of Cumberland's second major contribution: he also bred perhaps the most famous thoroughbred of all, the peerless Eclipse.

In 1763 Cumberland authorized the mating of the mare Spiletta, an animal who had never won and bought from Sir Robert Eden, with his own stallion, Marske. Marske, bred by John Hutton in Yorkshire, had been acquired by Cumberland as a result of a swap. Hutton had taken a chestnut Arabian in exchange for Marske. The duke raced Marske and, although he won the Jockey Club Plate at Newmarket over a distance in excess of 3 miles 6 furlongs, he was by no stretch of the imagination a top class racehorse. In fact he won only two more races, one of which was a walkover. In a fit of inspiration Cumberland decided to give Marske a chance at stud at Cranbourne Lodge. From his rather unpromising union with Spiletta, he produced a chestnut colt, Eclipse, named after the great eclipse that occurred in 1764.

In 1765 Cumberland died from the effects of a war wound and excessive corpulence. He never saw the exploits of the progeny of his inspired mating. The duke's bloodstock was dispersed by Richard Tattersall and Eclipse was purchased by a Smithfield meat salesman, William Wildman for 75 gns. Wildman must have had some idea that Eclipse was a promising sort. On his arrival at the sale he found the horse had changed hands for 70 gns before the advertised time of sale. He insisted the colt should be resubmitted, and bought him.

Wildman gave his new acquisition plenty of time to develop. In 1769, Eclipse met four other rivals in a race that was to be run in three heats at Epsom. He won the first heat very easily. In the second heat he finished fully 240 yards in front of his four rivals, eliminating the need for the third heat to be run. An interested observer was the adventurer Dennis O'Kelly, who bought a half share in Eclipse a month later for 650 gns and in April 1770 bought the other half for a further 1,100 gns. It was he who uttered the immortal words 'Eclipse first, the rest nowhere' when assessing the prospects of the second heat. O'Kelly had made a worthwhile purchase. Eclipse was never beaten, winning eighteen races, including eleven King's Plates, of which seven were walkovers. Few owners were prepared to pitch their horses against him.

In 1771, Eclipse was retired to the Clay Hill Stud near Epsom at a fee of 50 gns. The fee was not maintained, and for the rest of his career it varied from 20 to 30 gns. Eclipse died of colic on 27 February 1789, having sired the winners of 862 races, worth £158,047. Eclipse sired three Derby winners during his time at stud and a single Oaks winner. The main characteristics of his progeny were their speed and early maturity. Breeders of the time were quick to realize that Eclipse and Herod mixed in any pedigree produced exactly what is required in the perfect racehorse, the right blend of stamina and speed. Incredibly, the two horses bred at Windsor by the Duke of Cumberland proved to be totally complementary in terms of the hereditary characteristics they passed on to their progeny. The Herod/Eclipse cross is found in the pedigrees of Sergeant, Skyscraper, John Bull, Waxy, Spread Eagle, Archduke, Champion, Whalebone and Whisker: all early Derby winners and fathers of the future.

To complement his breeding operation Cumberland maintained a personal racing stable. Unlike his royal predecessors he was a great advocate of the downland areas of Berkshire for bringing his horses to peak fitness. Charles II favoured the flat heathland of Newmarket, as did many of his courtiers. Cumberland maintained a racing stable at Kate's Gore, situated north of the village of East Ilsley. According to the nineteenth-century chronicler William Hewett, in his *History and Antiquities of the Hundred of Compton*, the Duke had 'here a range of commodious stables, built by the Duke for his running horses, which were kept here for training on the neighbouring downs'. Hewett also wrote: 'If Eclipse was not foaled at Kate's Gore, which is more than probable, certain it is that he was here in training as a yearling; and that on the neighbouring downs, it was that this most wonderful horse first acquired and displayed that extraordinary speed which in after life rendered him so remarkable.' Eclipse was certainly foaled at Windsor Forest, but it is perfectly possible that he learnt the rudiments of his craft as a yearling on the Ilsley Downs. Herod, foaled some six years earlier, is likely to have been prepared for his races at Kate's Gore.

Hewett reported that the Prince of Wales wished to purchase the stables on his uncle Cumberland's death but John Head, the duke's landlord, had been so appalled by the behaviour of Cumberland's stable staff that according to Hewett he 'levelled the premises to the ground'. Ironically it was not until the present Queen's time that royal racehorses were trained on the Ilsley Downs again. Cumberland designed a racecourse on Prestall Down near to his stables, but it was a short-lived project. Hewett claimed that it was 'destroyed by plough' around 1800.

Country meetings were a feature of most counties at the time, and Berkshire was no exception. Originally races were run as matches, with the two owners putting up the purse and the winner taking the proceeds. Gradually this form of racing lost favour due to its private nature: races with several runners were far more exciting. The invention of the King's Plates by Charles II, with the rules and regulations that accompanied them, set the form for a different sort of racing. The King's Plates were initially for horses of six years old and over, the runners carrying 12 stone. The races were run in four heats over 4 miles, and the winner of any two heats was the victor. From 1751, four- and five-year-olds were deemed eligible to run in King's Plates, although Newmarket's first ever four-year-old race was run in in 1744. In 1756 three-year-old racing was introduced at Newmarket. By 1786 a two-year-old event was on the Newmarket card. With this age reduction came a reduction in weight to be carried, as well as in the distance of the races themselves. In the first half of the eighteenth century there were few formal rules outside the King's Plates. The formation of the Jockey Club, a self-elected body of prominent and leading racing men, in 1750, created an authoritative body to control the sport that had been absent since the death of Tregonwell Frampton in 1727. The importance of the Jockey Club grew so rapidly that by 1758 it was the arbitrator of disputes at all courses other than Newmarket. The Club has remained the controlling voice of racing to the present day.

By 1740 racing had assumed huge popularity countrywide. However, the gambling that went hand in hand with it had begun to worry both its royal patrons and the government of the day. In 1740 the Duke of Bolton put forward an ingenious piece of legislation that became law. An act was passed to 'restrain and prevent the excessive increase of horse races'. The object of this was to eliminate officially the minor meetings that had sprung up around the country, as they were deemed undesirable socially and bad for the bloodstock breed. The means to this end were created by a rider in the act, stating that the minimum value of a race should be £50, except at Newmarket or Black Hambleton in Yorkshire. The legislation had the desired effect, and many small meetings perished.

In Berkshire, several courses survived as they were able to put on races for the specified amount. In 1750 Reading had a three-day meeting on Bulmersh Heath. Records exist of the 1754 card, which included a £50 plate for aged hunters 'that never won five pounds, but such as have been actually used as hunters last season; and not such as were only hunted a few times on purpose to be called so'.

Maidenhead also held a two-day September meeting on a course next to Maidenhead Thicket. The 1754 card included an event with the statutory £50 purse for horses of 'fourteen hands to carry nine stone: all over or under to be allowed weights for inches, according to the Rules of the Sporting: to be measured in four foot and a half of chalk with their heads over a table'. Thousands watched the sport. In 1768 the King of Denmark attended the races at Maidenhead and in 1767 Mrs Philip Libbye Powys, a famous hostess of the day, wrote in her diary: 'We went to Maidenhead races the middle day, the whole royal family there'.

Extra entertainment at these fixtures included cock fighting, not outlawed until 1840, held at the Golden Bear Inn at Reading and also at the Red Lion at Lambourn, which held an annual meeting in the 1750s. The 1771 May card consisted of three £50 plates, one given by the Lord Craven of the day, the principal landowner of the area. An interesting condition for the meeting was that no EO (an early form of roulette) tables were to be allowed on the race down, or in the town of Lambourn. Lord Craven was also in evidence as a sponsor of races held on Letcombe Downs above Wantage.

At Abingdon, now in Oxfordshire, on Culham Heath, one of the most successful country meetings was held. A commentator of the day described the course as 'most judiciously laid out, both as a fine piece of racing ground, and also for affording diversion to the company, as the horses may be seen quite round from an easy occasion without moving from the spot'.

Newbury hosted a two-day meeting in August 1805 on a new course on Enborne Heath to the south of the town 'by the kind permission of the Earl of Craven'. The card included a Maiden Plate of £50, a Free Plate of £50, a Handicap Plate of £50 and a Hunters Sweepstakes of 5 gns each. The meeting was reputedly a success, *The Times* commenting: 'This being the first year of Newbury races on the new course, they have been attended by all the rank and fashion of the county.' However, racing only lasted at Enborne Heath until 1811. Permission was then sought from the Earl of Carnarvon for a new course at Woodhay Heath where meetings took place until 1815, a Gold Cup of 100 guineas being run for in that year.

In 1682 a meeting 'on which was betted 500 guinnys' was held at Datchet Ferry, a town on the Thames east of Windsor. In 1705, the diarist Narcissus Luttrell wrote: 'The royal couple [Anne and Prince George of Denmark] seem mightily given to racing. The Queen has appointed horse races to be held at Datchet after her return from Winchester to Windsor'. In 1709 Luttrell commented: 'Yesterday was a great horse race at Datchet. Colonel Moreton won the Queen's Plate and the Earl of Bridgwater the Town of Windsor Plate.' Datchet, although the earliest recorded meeting in Berkshire, does not seem to feature after this. The reason is that in 1710, after a particularly enjoyable gallop in a light chaise following the Royal Buckhounds, Queen Anne determined to have a racecourse built on Ascot Heath, which she thought the perfect venue for a racecourse. She put her Master of the Buckhounds, the Duke of Somerset, in charge of its constitution, creating a precedent. For a further 190 years the Master of the Buckhounds was in charge of racing at Ascot.

The course the Duke designed was simple and cheap. The racecourse itself cost the princely sum of £588 19s 5d, paid to a William Lowe. The carpenter, William Erlybrown, was paid £15 2s 8d for fixing the posts, which were painted by Benjamin Chalchott for £2 15s. On 11 August 1711, the first day's racing was held on a Saturday, incorporating a £50 Plate. On the following Monday they raced for a £100 Queen's Plate. A second meeting was held on 17 and 18 September that year. In 1714 racing was cancelled after the queen died. Ascot raced on a minor scale, having a three-day meeting in 1735 and 1736, and after only one day's racing in 1739, the course, closed until 1744. Strangely, it was the victim of the Duke of Bolton's restriction of minor meetings act.

The Duke of Cumberland, in his capacity of Ranger for Windsor Forest, took the racecourse under his wing and revived its fortunes. By the time of his death in 1765, the future of Ascot was secure. In 1768 the June five-day meeting was held, as it is in the present day. In 1791 the Oatlands Stakes, reputedly the first ever handicap, was run for a first prize of 2,950 gns. The Derby of that year was only worth £1,079 5s to the winner.

While Ascot thrived with the aid of continued royal patronage, many of Berkshire's other courses were forced to close in the early years of the nineteenth century. The Enclosure Acts of the first years of the century caused much common land to pass into private ownership. Enborne Heath was enclosed in 1811 and Reading's Bulmersh Heath in 1816, while Lambourn suffered in this respect also. The course on Weathercock Downs held its last meeting in 1803, surviving thirty years longer than the Letcombe Downs course above Wantage. Maidenhead held its last regular meeting as early as 1787, although a short-lived revival occurred for only one year in 1801. Cumberland's course at Ilsley was ploughed up in the first decade of the nineteenth century. Reading held its last fixture in 1814, and it was not until 1845 that racing was revived at a new venue on King's Meadow. The last recorded fixture at Woodhay Heath, Newbury, took place in 1815. Mostly these meetings proved not to be financially viable, as in the main they were only annual affairs. By 1815, the year of Waterloo, Berkshire had only two surviving courses, Ascot and Abingdon.

In 1838 the Great Western Railway reached Maidenhead. There is no doubt that this increased the attendance at Ascot, where a new grandstand was finished in 1839. Coaches were run to and from the course to carry the crowds which came from London by train. Almost certainly the benefits that Ascot incurred prompted Reading to attempt a revival of the fixture that had been terminated in 1814. With the Great Western established at Reading by 1843, a new course was opened on King's Meadow, attractively positioned between the Thames and the newly constructed line. The sport appeared to thrive, and a year later the meeting was extended to a two-day fixture. In 1872 a local paper was to report that the sport was 'first rate'. In 1874 the short-lived revival failed. After only thirty years, racing ended on King's Meadow. The promoter, a Mr Tompkins, sadly concluded that although the attendance was as large as it had ever been since the new course opened, he was getting a poor return on his investment and was finding great difficulty in arranging a fixture date.

For a few years in the 1840s, a two-day meeting was held on Hungerford Common. There was then a break of ten years before John Clerke Free, the landlord of the Three Swans public house, engineered a revival. In 1866 the card included the Hungerford Stakes, the forerunner of the important Newbury race of the present day. But Mr Clerke Free was to experience the same difficulties as his colleague at Reading, and although a special train was advertised for the 1869 fixture, the meeting closed soon afterwards. It is ironic that the railway, which brought the large crowds to Ascot in the 1840s, was to be the death knell for the smaller country meetings. As the network grew, racegoers found it easier to get to the better meetings further afield, so the country meetings became less popular and many folded. As well as Reading and Hungerford, Abingdon was to close in 1875.

Steeplechasing was to become increasingly popular throughout the nineteenth century. In 1826 only one steeplechase course was recorded as being in existence. Yet by 1842 there were forty-two recognized venues.

The Three Swans, Hungerford. The landlord John Clerke Free was responsible for the revival of racing on Hungerford Common in the 1860s

Several small courses appeared in Berkshire. In 1840 a four mile steeple-chase was run near Newbury. Reports exist of a steeplechase meeting at Whiteknights Park near Reading in 1859. In 1861 a meeting was held in April near Windsor. A court diarist reported that Queen Victoria attended, but left suddenly, appalled by the language of a rider who had a heavy fall well within her Majesty's earshot. Records of these early events are very vague, as the sport did not gain official recognition until the formation of the National Hunt Committee in 1866.

These early jumping courses appear to have had short careers in the main. Two later additions proved sufficiently popular to survive into the twentieth century. At Maiden Erlegh, John Hargreaves, a master of the South Berks Hunt, founded a course where hunt and yeomanry races, similar to the modern hunter chases, were run. Maiden Erlegh was bought in 1903 by Solly Joel, who allowed racing to continue until the First World War. Hawthorn Hill near Winkfield was originally started in 1887. Designed originally for local farmers, who allowed the Buck-hounds to run over their land, it was soon being used by the military to hold meetings and became a mecca for this type of rider. Two three-day meetings, in the spring and November of the year, proved so popular that they became part of the conventional calendar. The April Household Brigade meeting, open only to amateur riders, also proved a great attraction. The popular course did not survive the Second World War, holding its last meeting in 1939. Ascot, Windsor, founded in 1866 on its present Rays Meadow site in a crook of the Thames below the town and New-bury, founded by John Porter, the renowned Kingsclere trainer, survive and flourish today, and will be discussed in detail in later chapters.

The status of trainers at the beginning of the nineteenth century was not high. Indeed, they were generally referred to as 'training grooms'. The great jockey Sam Chifney, who was retained by the Prince of Wales in the 1790s, wrote in his autobiography: 'In 1775 I could train horses for running better than any person I ever yet saw. Riding I learnt myself, and training I learnt from Mr Richard Prince, training groom to Lord Foley.' Not much credit and probably not much reward went with this employment. Robert Robson, who was the most distinguished trainer of this period, did much to improve the lot of his profession and increase its social standing. Known rather grandly as 'The Emperor of Trainers', Robson ran by far the most successful stable of the first quarter of the nineteenth century. In 1793, as private trainer to Sir Frederick Poole at

Lewes, he had won the Derby with Waxy. His move to Newmarket soon afterwards saw his career really take off.

At Newmarket Robson enjoyed the patronage of the third Duke of Grafton, one of the principal breeders of the day, winning the Derby for him on three occasions with Tyrant, Pope and Whalebone. He won three further Derbys during his career, with Whisker in 1815 for the fourth Duke of Grafton, Azor for Mr Payne in 1817 and Emilius for J.R. Udney in 1823. Robson's successes in the Newmarket Classics were even more incredible. Between 1819 and 1827 he won the 2,000 Guineas five times for the fourth Duke and the 1,000 eight times. Robson was known for more delicate handling of his horses than most of his contemporaries: none of his seven Derby winners were raced at two. As well as perfecting the art of training, he did much to establish racehorse training as a definitive profession. His achievements improved the status of the trainer: no more was he a glorified groom. Robson retired in 1828, and was presented with a plate as a testimonial of his ability and integrity by the members of the Jockey Club. The trainer was now an officially recognized professional.

After Robson's retirement the Malton, Yorkshire trainer, John Scott took on the mantle of the country's most successful trainer. His Whitewall stable was patronized by many of the country's leading owners. Scott, who was born at Chippenham near Newmarket, where his father trained for two confidantes of the Prince Regent, Sir John Lade and Sir H. Featherstone, bought the Whitewall stables in 1825. He had worked previously for the Epsom trainer James Edwards, and as private trainer for a Mr Thomas Houldsworth, who had a dozen or so horses at Rockhill in the confines of Sherwood Forest. His first important owner was Edward Petre, who had known Scott when he had worked for James Croft at Glasgow House, Middleham. Scott was quick to establish himself, winning three St Legers in a row for Petre with Matilda in 1827, The Colonel in 1828, and Rowton Scott in 1829. Other important owners followed rapidly, keen to jump on the bandwagon.

Lord Derby, the prime minister, Lord Chesterfield, the Marquess of Westminster and John Bowes, who owned West Australian, the first winner of the triple crown (all three Classic races), numbered among Scott's owners. At the zenith of his career Scott had a hundred horses in training at Whitewall. The fact that only 1,000 were in training throughout the country at the time shows the extent of Scott's dominance of the sport.

Between 1827 and 1871, when he died as a result of a chill caught while watching his string exercise on Stockton racecourse, Scott trained forty-one Classic winners.

Scott revolutionized the training of the racehorse, maintaining three separate gallops to condition his charges. As well as the famous Langton Wolds at Malton, he used a gallop at Pigburn near Doncaster, when the ground became too firm at Malton. He also rented accommodation and gallops for his horses at Leatherhead, from where he dispatched his formidable raiding parties for the big summer southern fixtures, such as Epsom and Ascot. The massive strength in depth of his string ensured that Yorkshire became the fashionable training place of the period. John Barham Day, the father of the famous racing family, was the first southern trainer who gave Scott any competition.

Day, born at Houghton Down in Hampshire, was the son of a small country trainer John Day. Rather surprisingly, as his father reputedly weighed more than 20 stone, Day, like several of his brothers, became a jockey, and a lightweight one at that. For virtually all of his career he was able to ride at the featherweight of 7 stone. In his youth he scratched a living around the small Hampshire meetings. Not until Day attracted the attention of the fourth Duke of Grafton and his trainer, Robert Robson, did he have the chance to pit his skills against the best of the day, such as Frank Buckle at the major meetings. It was as a relative unknown that he rode a Classic double for the Duke and Robson in 1826 on Dervise in the 2,000 Guineas and Problem in the fillies' equivalent. He won two further Classics for the Duke in the Oaks of 1828 and 1831 on Turquoise and Oxygen. He also rode as lightweight jockey for King George IV, winning the Somersetshire Stakes at Bath in 1831 on the king's Maria.

In 1835, Day was sufficiently established to return to Hampshire to train at Danebury, near Stockbridge. For a time he continued to ride most of his stable inmates. Throughout his riding career Day had been a heavy gambler, and was quite prepared to deceive the connections of the horses he rode as to their ability to obtain for himself a better price. He was also quite prepared for any horse he trained or rode to perform below its capacity, if he was to accrue financial advantage from it being beaten.

A most notable example of this occurred when Day was training privately for the moneylender Henry Padwick at Michel Grove in Sussex, towards the end of his career. Padwick had heavily backed his 2,000

Guineas entrant Sir Hubert down to favouritism. His only serious rival appeared to be Lord of the Isles, trained by John Barham Day's son, William at Woodyates in Wiltshire. Father and son got together and decided that to give Lord of the Isles a clear passage in the Guineas, John Day should give Sir Hubert a light preparation to get him beaten. All this was without Padwick's knowledge. The plan worked, and Lord of the Isles beat Sir Hubert by a neck at Newmarket. Soon afterwards Padwick discovered how he had lost his money, and dismissed John Day from his position.

When Day started at Danebury, his first important patron was Lord George Bentinck. Sir George's main ambition was to be the most successful punter and owner on the turf. He was quite prepared to spend a large degree of his fortune on Danebury to fulfil this desire. He built new stables and laid out new gallops to enable Day to meet these objectives. Bentinck and Day were most successful winning the 1,000 Guineas with Chapeau d'Espagne in 1837 and the 2,000 a year later with Grey Momus. The outstanding animal that John Day trained for Lord George was Crucifix, who won the 1,000, 2,000 and Oaks. He also rode the mare in her Classic triumphs. The rather tempestuous relationship between Bentinck and Day ended in 1841. Day's son William had written to Lord George encouraging him to back a stable inmate with confidence, but

Danebury, the headquarters of the famous training family the Days, ancestors of Lester Piggott

had also written to a bookmaker telling him to lay Bentinck the horse as it could not win. Unfortunately for John Day, William placed the letters in the wrong envelopes! Bentinck removed his horses to John Kent at Goodwood and conducted a vendetta against the Day family for the rest of his life.

John Barham Day left Danebury a few years later to take up Henry Padwick's appointment, and handed over the stables to his son John, who maintained its formidable success. Like his father before him he had no regard for his owners if he could further his own interests. He bankrupted the young Marquess of Hastings by allowing him to back the filly Lady Elizabeth for the Derby of 1868, knowing full well she would never recover her form after a particularly arduous two-year-old campaign of thirteen races. Day was suspected to have laid Lady Elizabeth every time Hastings had backed her.

Although John Barham Day may not have done much to further the integrity of what was, even before his time, perceived as a less than honest sport, he had proved that horses of the highest class could be trained on the high chalk downs of the southern counties. The southern training areas, somewhat upstaged by the phenomenal successes of John Scott on Yorkshire's Langton Wolds, and Robson before him on the flat heathland of Newmarket, were to rise to prominence from the 1850s onwards. The steep downland hills of the southern counties were to become increasingly fashionable for conditioning the racehorse. Berkshire was to figure prominently in this revival.

2
THE DEVELOPMENT OF BERKSHIRE RACING UP TO 1945

Berkshire's first Derby winner, Wild Dayrell, was bred at Littlecote, on the banks of the River Kennet a few miles from Hungerford, by Francis Popham, a country squire. It was somewhat fortunate for Berkshire that she can claim the credit for his victory. His early two-year-old career was so unpromising that Popham bought him back from Lord Henry Lennox, who had purchased him as a yearling, for 250 gns.

Popham's bloodstock breeding was more a hobby than a business. He had bought Wild Dayrell's dam Ellen Middleton on the advice of his stud groom, Rickaby, from the Lord Zetland of the day for only 50 gns. Popham sent Ellen Middleton to the stallion, Ion, who had been second in Amato's Derby. In time she produced Wild Dayrell, named after a former owner of Littlecote, who had killed a baby by throwing it into a fire. He was the first foal ever to be born at Littlecote.

Born shortly after midnight, Wild Dayrell was greeted by the unlikely figure of Popham's butler in his nightcap, who then proceeded to load the newborn foal into a wheelbarrow to move it to a warmer stable. The butler is reputed to have exclaimed with a certain degree of clairvoyance that he wished 'to wheel the winner of the Derby once in my life'. On his return to his cottage, Rickaby, the stud groom, saw a wild duck and drake sitting together on a hedge. He believed this to be an omen that the little foal would prove to be a famous horse.

After Lord Henry Lennox had tired of his purchase, Wild Dayrell returned to his birthplace and Popham sold a share to his friend, Lord Craven, who lived at Ashdown House not far from Lambourn. He was trained by Rickaby in the Littlecote water meadows. Presumably he showed his groom some talent, for soon he was moved to Ashdown Park with two other stablemates to take advantage of the better training facilities that Lord Craven's home and the surrounding downland could offer.

In the autumn of his two-year-old days, Wild Dayrell was deemed ready to run. He was despatched to Newmarket, where he won a minor

The road from Lambourn to Upper Lambourn in Victorian days

event from only two opponents. This was to be his only race at two and, more strangely, he never ran again before his Derby triumph of 1855. As a three-year-old, Wild Dayrell gave cause for optimism for Epsom. He pulverized his lead horses to such a degree in his gallops on the Downs that many broke down. Robert Sherwood, the Epsom jockey, was engaged for the Derby and was reputedly very impressed by the way his mount performed in a trial ten days before the race.

Although Wild Dayrell had not appeared in public since his two-year-old days, rumours of his class had reached the country's racecourses. As a result he was heavily backed for the Derby. Suspiciously, the bookmakers continued to field him at generous prices, even though they stood to lose a fortune if he won. Francis Popham heard that Wild Dayrell was going to be prevented from winning and immediately sacked a stable-hand, who was rumoured to be part of this villainous plan.

Further complications arose, however. Popham was approached by a man who offered him the then very considerable sum of £5,000, if he scratched Wild Dayrell from the Derby. Popham also discovered that the horse van that was to take Wild Dayrell to Epsom had been tampered with. When he tested it, with a bullock aboard, to his horror a wheel fell off. When the gang who had tried to stop Wild Dayrell running at

Epsom realized that their efforts had been thwarted, they began to back him for the race, rather than their previous fancy Kingstown, who was owned by a particularly shady bookmaker, Harry Hill, whom Popham was sure had been behind the earlier sabotage attempts.

Such was the weight of money that the gang invested that Wild Dayrell started an even money favourite for the Derby. Sherwood had plenty in hand, and won by an easy two lengths from Kingstown. Popham was apparently so appalled by the skulduggery that he declared he never wished to own a Derby runner again. Wild Dayrell later won York's Ebor St Leger, but broke down when contesting the Doncaster Cup. He never ran again and was retired to stud.

Wild Dayrell's achievement in winning the Derby without a previous outing that year did much to draw racing's attention to his training place on the Lambourn Downs. From then on, owners sought to send their charges to be prepared on the turf where Popham's colt had reached peak fitness for his Epsom triumph. Soon stables sprang up around Lambourn and the rest of Berkshire's downland: Wild Dayrell's win attracted the public's attention to the area, which was soon to rival Newmarket for prominence in the thoroughbred world.

Further east, south of the Ridgeway, East Ilsley, famous previously as a sheep market and in the eighteenth century the Duke of Cumberland's chosen training place, was making its mark in the thoroughbred world. James Dover, originally a head lad to the Hednesford, Staffordshire trainer, Samuel Lord, assembled a formidable stable. Among his patrons were Sir Richard Sutton, General Pearson and Lord Rosebery. In 1866, Dover won the triple crown with Lord Lyon, and in 1867 the 1,000 Guineas and the St Leger with the colt's full sister, Achievement. Bred by General Mark Pearson at Oakley Hall, Kettering, Lord Lyon's grandam, Ellen Horne, a filly by Redshank, had been bought by Pearson as a hack for his wife for only 18 gns. Early in his two-year-old career, Lord Lyon had shown Dover he had exceptional ability. When galloped with his three-year-old half sister, Gardevisure, he had performed so well that Dover chose the leading two-year-old race, the Champagne Stakes at Doncaster, for his debut. Lord Lyon dead-heated with Redan for the Champagne but did not contest the run off. After victories at Newmarket in the Troy and Criterion Stakes, Lord Lyon went into winter quarters a leading contender for the 1866 Classic races.

Lord Lyon's spring work was so impressive at Ilsley that he was sent off the odds-on favourite for the 2,000 Guineas, even though he was part-nered by one of Dover's work riders, Thomas. Harry Custance, his regular rider, was injured at the time. Under his young rider he won the Newmarket Classic beating Monarch of the Glen. Odds-on again for the Derby, with Custance back in the saddle, he had to be hard ridden to dispose of Savernake. At Ascot he was beaten in the Prince of Wales Stakes by the Derby third, Rustic. Taken home and freshened up by Dover, Lord Lyon was back to his best in September for the St Leger meeting. He again beat his old rival Savernake in a close finish by the narrowest of margins. Lord Lyon won two good races at Newmarket in the autumn of his three-year-old career, and also disposed of Rustic, who had beaten him that summer at Ascot, in a £1,000 match.

Campaigned heavily as a four-year-old, Lord Lyon won six races in a row, including the Ascot Biennial. In all Lord Lyon won seventeen of his twenty-one races for over £26,000 worth of prize money, before being retired to stud at the end of his four-year-old career. Strangely, Custance did not rate Lord Lyon a great horse. He described him as having a slight wind infirmity and discernibly whistling in his races. He believed that Lord Lyon was not a true stayer, and somewhat lucky in this respect to have won a triple crown.

Such was Dover's reputation as a trainer that he was chosen by perhaps the greatest Victorian trainer of all, John Porter of Kingsclere, to take charge of several horses in 1865, when Porter suffered a serious illness. Other distinguished names were present nearby at this time. Indeed, three members of the famous Scottish Dawson family trained at Ilsley and neighbouring Compton in the early stages of their careers, before their moves to Newmarket and further fame.

Sons of the famous Scottish trainer, George Dawson, who prepared his horses around what is now Gullane golf course south-east of Edinburgh on the Firth of Forth, made a tremendous impact on the turf in the second half of the nineteenth century. Between 1853 and 1895 three of George Dawson's sons, Mat, Joseph and John trained a staggering thirty-seven Classic winners between them. To add to the record, John Dawson's son George, who took over his uncle Mat's Heath House, Newmarket stable, trained a further ten before the turn of the century. Their eldest brother Tom, who trained at Middleham, won a further five Classics. He is generally credited with being the first trainer to prepare horses without sweating them by clothing them in heavy rugs at exercise. This practice was discontinued soon afterwards, although Tom's brother Joseph was reputed to have been the laughing stock of Newmarket when he repeated the practice there. His subsequent success soon caused his detractors to laugh on the other side of their faces.

In 1846, after the death of his father, Mathew Dawson left Scotland permanently to take up an appointment to train horses and manage the stud of Lord John Scott. Although Lord John's stud was based near Rugby he maintained a racing stable at Compton in Berkshire. Mat

Mat Dawson, the legendary Newmarket trainer, who started his career at Yew Tree Cottage Stables, Compton, in 1846

Dawson was not long in winning some good prizes for Lord John and his partner, Sir John Don-Wauchope. In 1851 he won Ascot's New Stakes and the July Stakes at Newmarket, two of the principal two-year-old races, with Hobbie Noble. In 1853 he won the first of his twenty-eight Classic races with a brown filly, Catherine Hayes, who beat Dove in the Oaks. All his life Dawson rated Catherine Hayes as one of the best mares he had ever handled. In 1857, when Lord John Scott retired from racing, Dawson sold his remaining racing interests to the Scottish iron magnate, James Merry, who had bought Hobbie Noble as a two-year-old. Dawson agreed to move, vacating his Yew Tree Cottage stables for the private stables that Merry maintained at Russley Park, some 4 miles west of Lambourn, in Wiltshire. Success was quick to follow. In 1858 Dawson won the Leger with Merry's Sunbeam and two years later his first Derby with Thormanby. By 1866 Dawson and Merry had parted company, and the trainer had moved to Newmarket where his career was to reach new heights, training a further twenty-six Classic winners, many of which were ridden by Fred Archer.

Dawson's brothers were not long in moving to Newmarket either. John Dawson left Roden House, Compton in the 1870s to train for Prince Batthyany at Warren House, winning the 1875 Derby with Galopin. Joseph had vacated his East Ilsley stables for Newmarket earlier to be private trainer for the Earl of Stamford. By 1861 he had won the 2,000 Guineas for his patron, with Diophantus. Another East Ilsley trainer of the time to move to Newmarket was Jem Godding. When Macaroni won the Derby of 1863, Godding put Newmarket back into fashion. For some years previously Newmarket had been plagued by dry summers, with the ground on the famous Limekilns gallops being firm by the beginning of May. Many owners of the day had moved their horses to be trained on the better ground of the southern downlands. Godding declared that if he could not train a Derby winner on the Limekilns he could not train one anywhere. Macaroni proved him right, and New-market again became a thriving training centre. The fact that all the Dawsons moved to Newmarket soon after is proof positive that Godding's achievement did much to restore principal owners' faith in the heathland training grounds. In this respect, Godding's win at Epsom with Macaroni was Berkshire's loss. William Stevens prepared the 1887 Derby winner Merry Hampton at Compton, but two weeks before the race George Baird, who raced under the name of Mr Abington, sent the horse back to his private trainer, Martin Gurry, at Newmarket. Baird had quarrelled with Gurry in the winter of 1886 and sent his whole string to Stevens at Compton. As a result of Baird's unpredictable behaviour, which was characteristic of the man, Stevens missed the chance of appearing in the record books as trainer of a Derby winner, although he had been responsible for virtually all of Merry Hampton's training schedule. Stevens's achievement was all the more considerable as Merry Hampton had never set foot on a racecourse before his Derby triumph.

Lambourn was holding its own as well. In 1861 a huge chestnut colt named Kettledrum had been sent from Lancashire to contest the 2,000 Guineas. Reputedly only half trained due to trouble with his teeth, he had run a marvellous race, finishing second to the Joseph Dawson-trained, Diophantus. His owner, Colonel Towneley, decided then that Kettledrum's Derby preparation should be concluded somewhere other than the Lancashire moors near Bolton, where his trainer George Oates exercised his horses. Towneley chose the Seven Barrows establishment of the trainer Prince, 2 miles east of Lambourn. Oates travelled south with Kettledrum, and remained in sole charge of the horse's Derby preparation. Kettledrum enjoyed the Berkshire air and worked so well that he was a well backed 12–1 chance when he lined up for the Derby.

A nineteenth-century view of Lambourn

Kettledrum, ridden by the northern jockey Bullock, was a lucky winner. The favourite Dundee, trained at Russley by Mat Dawson, broke down when two lengths clear in the final furlong. Bullock saw his chance and drove Kettledrum past the injured favourite to win by a length. Kettledrum's guineas conquerer, Diophantus, finished a further neck away in third.

Kettledrum was below his best in the St Leger, and was just beaten by Caller Ou, whom ironically George Oates had tried to buy as a yearling. Two days later Kettledrum was asked to concede a massive 16 lb. to his Lambourn neighbour and Oaks winner, Brown Duchess, trained by Joseph Saxon in the Doncaster Cup. He ran a marvellous race to dead-heat with the daughter of The Flying Dutchman, but such were his exertions that he never raced again. 1861 had been a golden year with the Berkshire village plundering the two Epsom Classic races. However, it was a further thirty years before Lambourn was to celebrate another Classic success. In 1890 Seven Barrows was again the establishment to produce Lambourn's next Classic winner.

Charles Jousiffe, who was master of Seven Barrows at the time, was a large thickset happy-go-lucky figure of a man, who unlike some trainers of his era was open if he fancied one of his charges. He also knew if he had a good horse in his yard, having won many good races including the Cambridgeshire, the first ever Eclipse and the Hardwicke at Ascot with the high class Bendigo in the 1880s. In 1889 Jousiffe had plundered several top class two-year-old races with a big powerful bay colt by Wisdom named Surefoot, owned by a young Guards officer, Archie Merry. Jousiffe made no secret of the fact that he thought Surefoot would win the 2,000 Guineas, and provide him with a first Classic winner.

Jousiffe was proved correct. Although many paddock judges thought Surefoot looked too fat in the preliminaries, he scored easily in the Newmarket Classic and went to the Derby an odds-on favourite with his trainer believing he could not be beaten. However, temperament, which was to trouble him in later life got the better of him, and he ran fourth behind Sainfoin. Sainfoin's trainer, John Porter, had fancied him so little before the race that he had advised the horse's previous owner to sell. Jousiffe was reputedly so overwhelmed by Surefoot's defeat that in the spring of 1891 he was dead, although it should be added that he had suffered from a weak heart for some years!

On Jousiffe's death the Irishman Garrett Moore, who won the 1879 Grand National riding his own horse The Liberator, took over the stables

Lambourn House in James Chandler's day. Chandler trained the 1903 1,000 Guineas winner, Quintessence

with his head lad Baines nominally trainer. Surefoot was then showing signs of such ill temper that Moore is reported to have said to a friend: 'One of us had to be master and it was not going to be Surefoot.' Moore was successful, and Surefoot produced the best performance of his career to account for Common and Memoir in the 1892 Eclipse stakes. By the turn of the century Moore had left the Seven Barrows stable and for some time it ceased to be a racing establishment.

In 1903 the Lambourn trainer James Chandler won the 1,000 Guineas, with Lord Falmouth's Quintessence ridden by Herbert Randall. Randall had an unlikely background for a flat race jockey, being the son of a rich Northampton shoe manufacturer. Randall weighed only 8 stone, and after much early success was given permission to ride against professionals by the stewards. By 1902 he had turned professional, and in the same year he won the 2,000, 1,000 and Oaks on the great filly Sceptre. He was replaced for her Leger victory as the owner, Robert Sievier blamed him for her only Classic defeat in the Derby. Quintessence was a fortunate winner, as the second, Sun Rose, beaten only by one-and-a-half lengths, was affected by a malfunctioning starting gate and was badly impeded.

In 1897 Dick Dawson left his native Ireland to train at Whatcombe, an establishment south of Wantage, a few miles across the downs from Lambourn. At the beginning of Dawson's time at Whatcombe his head lad McNaughton was the nominal trainer. Drogheda, who won the 1898 Grand National, accompanied Dawson from Ireland, and it is McNaughton who is credited in the record books as being the official trainer. Not long after Drogheda's victory, Dawson began to concentrate on flat racing with the stable's principal patron in the early days being the fifth Earl of Carnarvon, for whom Dawson won the Royal Hunt Cup at Ascot as early as 1902. Two years later Dawson won the Doncaster Cup with Robert le Diable, for the same owner. During his early years at Whatcombe, Dawson shared the famous Woolley Down facilities with Henry Beardsley, who trained the fine stayer Prince Palatine to win the 1911 St Leger, as well as two Ascot Gold Cups, an Eclipse and a Coronation Cup.

At the outbreak of the First World War, Dawson left Whatcombe for Newmarket to take up an appointment as private trainer for Sir Edward Hulton. This move was to enhance Dawson's career in no uncertain terms. During the six years in Newmarket, Dawson won the 1916 substitute Derby and Oaks, run at Newmarket, with Sir Edward's Fifinella. He also came to the attention of the Newmarket trainer George Lambton, who was impressed by the way the studious and rather serious looking Irishman went about his business.

In 1921 the Aga Khan asked George Lambton to train for him, but Lambton's position as Lord Derby's private trainer at Stanley House made the proposition untenable. Lambton, however, consented to purchase yearlings for the Aga. When asked to recommend a trainer, he remembered being impressed by Dawson, and suggested to the Aga that he should send his horses to be trained at Whatcombe. Dawson had returned to Berkshire in 1919, unable to put up with Sir Edward Hulton's parsimonious nature any longer. Hulton had expected him to train his horses for £2 10s a week each, a task which Dawson found impossible. In 1922 Dawson took delivery of the first batch of Lambton's selected yearlings. Among them was the filly Cos, who provided Dawson with his first ever winner for the Aga in the Queen Mary at Royal Ascot. In 1923 the flying Mumtaz Mahal, by The Tetrarch, thrilled racegoers with her blinding speed, winning the National Breeders Produce Stakes, the Champagne and the Molecomb at Goodwood. Although Mumtaz

Mahal failed to stay the Guineas distance in 1923, finishing second to Plack, Dawson provided the Aga with his first two Classic wins in that year. Diophon won the 2,000 Guineas and Salmon Trout the St Leger. Mumtaz Mahal, brought back to sprinting, was supreme – winning the King George at Goodwood and the Nunthorpe at York. Dawson ended up leading trainer in the country with twenty-six winners worth £48,857.

In 1929 Dawson won the Derby with Mr Barnett's Trigo, a son of his stallion Blandford, one of the great sires of the early twentieth century. In 1930 Dawson prepared Blenheim to give the Aga a first Derby winner. Ridden by Harry Wragg, Blenheim was very much the stable's second string, Michael Beary the stable jockey electing to partner the Aga's other runner, Rustom Pasha. Blenheim beat Iliad by a length, with Rustom Pasha well beaten. Due to a training injury incurred after the Derby, Blenheim never ran again. All was not well despite the Derby winner. In 1931 the Aga removed his horses from Whatcombe, after a blinding row with his trainer at Newbury races, and sent them to the Newmarket stable of Frank Butters. Dawson, aged sixty-five when he broke with the Aga, continued to train in a small way at Whatcombe until his retirement in 1945. As a result of this argument Dawson was to lose the opportunity of training the Aga's 1935 triple crown winner, Barham.

Tom Cannon Junior, son of the Danebury trainer Tom Senior and grandson of John Day, trained at Compton after increasing weight had forced him to give up riding in 1889. In 1890 he won the Gimcrack at York with Garb d'Or and the 1900 Middle Park Stakes with the fast two-year-old Floriform. In 1905 he had the previous year's Derby winner St Amant at Hamilton House stables, and won the Jockey Club Stakes on his only outing from Compton. Cannon retired in 1936. Another former jockey who trained at Compton was Albert 'Snowy' Whalley who had stables at The Yews from his retirement from riding in 1924 until 1939. Whalley won the 1,000 Guineas on Roseway in 1919, and the 1920 Oaks on Charlebelle. Another resident there was Len Cundell, who won the Blackpool Steeplechase in 1905 at the now defunct Blackpool racecourse. Cundell later trained at Chilton, before the Air Ministry requisitioned the land to build a wartime airfield. Cundell subsequently moved further east in Oxfordshire to Aston Tirrold. At Ilsley, a mile away, Charles Peck, son of Robert Peck who trained Doncaster to win the 1873 Derby, trained privately for S.B. Joel for a brief period in the early

1900s. It was from Ilsley that he sent Bachelor's Button to beat the great race mare Pretty Polly in the Ascot Gold Cup of 1906. Mr Joel moved the stable to Newmarket soon after.

On his return from the First World War, Captain Richard Gooch started training in East Ilsley in 1919. Gooch thought that two-year-olds were too immature to train seriously but soon established a fine reputation as a trainer of stayers. After a move to Hodcott House in the neighbouring village of West Ilsley, he won the Goodwood Cup in 1928 and 1929 with Kinchinjunga and Old Orkney, the Chester Cup with Mountain Lad in 1930 and the Jockey Club Cup with Tatra in 1930. In 1928 Gooch broke his spine while hunting with the Quorn, and was crippled for the last ten years of his life. George Todd who later achieved tremendous success, started his training career in East Ilsley in 1928. In 1930 his string consisted of only four horses. By the start of the Second World War, however, the numbers had risen to twenty. Todd had the first of his many big race wins with stayers a year before he moved to the legendary Manton training establishment near Marlborough. He won the 1946 Chester Cup with Mr H.S. Lester's Retsel, whom he trained from Hodcott House, where he shared Captain Gooch's former yard with Gooch's successor Eric Stedall. Todd was so short of money when he

Captain Gooch's string passing the Harrow, West Ilsley in the years between the wars

started that he himself walked the sole inmate of his stable from Compton Station to East Ilsley. He had a large bet on his first ever runner, which was beaten. Undeterred he ran it two days later, doubled his bet and collected.

At Binfield Grove, near Bracknell, Norah Wilmot ran a thriving stable in the grounds of her home. Miss Wilmot, who had assisted her father, Sir Robert, for some twenty years before his death in 1931, was unable to claim official credit for her many victories until 1966. After a court case, the Jockey Club consented to grant licences to lady trainers. Miss Wilmot's head lads had held her licence before this, although she had been training winners for thirty-five years before. Miss Wilmot was a fine rider, and rode much exercise work in her early years. Mrs George Lambton recalled seeing Norah Wilmot and her sister Kathleen riding regularly on Newmarket Heath during the First World War, when Sir Robert moved his operation to Suffolk. Miss Wilmot trained two good stayers before the Second World War: in 1934 she won the Goodwood Cup with Loosestrife, and in 1937 the Doncaster Cup with Haulfryn.

About the same time that Dick Dawson was returning to Whatcombe from Newmarket, Harry Cottrill moved to Seven Barrows, Lambourn, the stable vacated by Garrett Moore at the turn of the century. Cottrill trained at the time of his move, in 1919, for Jimmy White, one of racing's most colourful characters. White, the son of a Rochdale bricklayer, had gone to London at the tender age of ten and later had made a large fortune speculating on the Stock Exchange. By 1927 he had lost it, and committed suicide at his home, King Edward Place, near Swindon. Although he later maintained a private stable at Foxhill near his home (Gordon Richards was apprenticed to one of his trainers, Martin Hartigan), Harry Cottrill was White's first ever trainer. In 1919 Irish Elegance, who had won the 1918 July Cup, landed the Royal Hunt Cup under the welter burden of 9 st. 11 lb., landing a massive gamble for White. Cottrill also provided White with another huge coup when Ivanhoe won the Cesarewitch at 100–6. In 1922 Cottrill won White the Lincoln with Granely. It is ironic that in 1927, the year of White's death, Cottrill was to saddle the first Classic winner from Seven Barrows since Surefoot won the 1890 2,000 Guineas. Adam's Apple won the Newmarket Classic for one of Cottrill's principal patrons, Sofer Whitburn. Ridden by Jack Leach, Adam's Apple was a surprise winner starting at 20–1. Adam's Apple was unplaced in Call Boy's Derby. By then he was rumoured to have wind problems, and was soon exported to Argentina to take up stallion duties.

Cottrill, like his predecessor Charles Jousiffe, was a cheerful figure and reputedly a great optimist as far as his horses' chances were concerned. He was, however, a great judge of a horse and passed on to his owners many cheap horses that proved to be bargains. In 1935 he bought Doreen Jane out of a selling race for only 360 gns. She was later to win the Ascot Stakes and the Northumberland Plate for her owner, the South African businessman Sir Abe Bailey. It was for Bailey that Cottrill saddled his only other Classic winner, when Lovely Rosa won the 1936 Oaks. Although a decent two-year-old, Lovely Rosa was thought not to have trained on after being unplaced in the Guineas. Allowed to take her chance at Epsom she was a surprise 33–1 winner in the hands of Tommy Weston. She never won again. In 1937 a serious fire ravaged Seven Barrows, and although Cottrill won the 1939 Hunt Cup for Sir Abe Bailey with Caerloptic, he retired from training at the start of hostilities.

While Seven Barrows thrived under Cottrill's tenure between the wars, so did the village of Lambourn 2 miles away. An Australian, Captain Ossie Bell, who had previously trained at Epsom, came to Delamere House, Lambourn with only a small army pension behind him. Victories in the Ebor Handicaps of 1922 and 1923 with Flint Jack soon enabled him to increase the size of his string. Although some of his contemporaries claimed his head lad did the training while he found the owners, jealousy was no doubt the cause of their assumption, as Bell increased the quality of his string. He soon attracted the attention of Sir Hugo Cunliffe-Owen, chairman of the British-American Tobacco Company. Sir Hugo liked to bet heavily at long prices, and there is no doubt that Bell kept him happy in this respect. Bell won the 1928 Derby with Felstead for Sir Hugo. Felstead, ridden by Harry Wragg, started at 33–1, his previous form appearing to be way below Derby standard. He had been only third in an Epsom Handicap before running a more promising sixth in the 2,000 Guineas. Felstead won the Derby comfortably by one-and-a-half lengths from Flamingo, after being brought with a characteristic late Wragg challenge. The favourite, Fairway, boiled over in the preliminaries and ran no race at all.

In 1938 Bell won the 1000 Guineas and Oaks with Felstead's daughter Rockfel. Rockfel, strangely, had started her racing career in the lowly company of a two-year-old Sandown seller where she finished only eighth. She improved throughout her juvenile year to record a victory in a York maiden, a performance that earned her the weight of 7 st. 10 lb. in the Free Handicap of the following year. She took her chance in the Free Handicap and finished third. Subsequently she won Epsom's Princess Elizabeth Stakes as a preparatory race for the 1,000 Guineas. On Guineas day she started as an 8–1 chance and was an easy winner under Sam Wragg. She started 3–1 favourite in the Oaks and this time, ridden by Sam Wragg's brother Harry, won easily in a fast time. In the autumn of the year she beat Pasch by five lengths in the Champion Stakes and was rated the equal of the Derby winner Bois Roussel in the Free Handicap of that year. Rockfel won the March Stakes as a four-year-old but was soon after retired to stud. She only bred one foal before dying of a twisted gut in 1941. He was the Hyperion horse Rockfella, sire of the 2,000 Guineas winner, Rockavon.

Rockfel proved a great bargain for her owner, Sir Hugo Cunliffe-Owen. He had bought her dam Rockcliffe for only 3,000 gns from another patron of Bell's stable, Lord Londonderry, when she was carrying Rockfel. Although Captain Bell died in 1949, his top hat and morning suit were purchased from a Lambourn tack sale by Paul Cole, who trained the 1991 Derby winner Generous. Cole greeted his early Royal Ascot winners in the Captain's suit and hat. He had invested in a new one by the time Generous won at Epsom!

The former jockey Fred Templeman, who won the 1919 Derby on Grand Parade for Lord Glanely, had been apprenticed to the Lambourn trainer John Hallick. In 1921 on Hallick's death he took over the trainer's stable Meridian on a small hill above the High Street in Lambourn. His principal patron was Lord Jersey, whose Greenback had finished second in the 1910 Derby. Lord Jersey died in 1923. In 1930 Templeman won the 2,000 Guineas for Sir Hugo Hirst with Diolite. Diolite was a top class two-year-old winning the Coventry and the Molecomb, and headed the Free Handicap of his year. He was a comfortable winner of the Guineas ridden by Freddie Fox. Starting favourite for the Derby he finished third to the Whatcombe-trained Blenheim but never showed form of that class again.

Templeman had another top class inmate at Meridian in 1933, the filly Chatelaine. After finishing seventh in the 1,000, she was a surprise winner of the Oaks at 25–1 ridden by Sam Wragg. She proved her victory was no fluke by dead-heating in the Champion Stakes with Dastur. Kept in training as a four-year-old, she did not regain her form. She fared even worse than Rockfel at stud, dying in her second year after producing a dead foal.

Templeman won a wartime 2,000 Guineas with the Fair Trial colt, Lambert Simnel, bred and owned by the Duke of Westminster. After finishing third in the Dewhurst as a two-year-old, Charlie Elliott steered him to victory in the 2,000. He ran unplaced behind Owen Tudor in the Derby and was unplaced also in the St Leger. Sold at the end of the season he was campaigned as a four-year-old, winning one of his two races and then retiring to stud. Templeman retired from training in 1956 and his yard is no longer a racing stable. He continued to live in Lambourn, until his death in 1973.

In 1930 the Maharajah of Rajpipla, after being introduced to Marcus Marsh at the Derby dinner of that year, instructed the young trainer to buy him a yearling. Marsh needed the order badly as he was down to only three horses in his newly built yard at Hodcott House. Marsh, having been sacked by his uncle Fred Darling for placing his bets personally rather than through Darling himself, had come to Hodcott to assist Captain Gooch, crippled by a hunting accident in 1928. By 1930 Sir Alfred Butt had set up Marsh as private trainer in the new yard next to Gooch's. The arrangement only lasted one year, with Butt, a notoriously difficult owner, who raced his horses consistently above their station and insisted on backing them to boot, removing his horses at the end of that season.

Marsh struggled through 1932 with his tiny string, and was asked by the Maharajah to buy a yearling to run in the Derby of 1934. Marsh bought the colt, which the Maharajah named Windsor Lad, for 1,300 gns. In 1933 Marsh had moved his operation to Lambourn, leasing the Delamere House yard from Ossie Bell, who had moved his larger string 200 yards away to Stork House. Windsor Lad won the Criterion Stakes at Newmarket in the autumn of his two-year-old days, and was alloted 8 st. 3 lb. in the Free Handicap. Windsor Lad thrived during the winter and was sent to run in the Chester Vase for his first outing of the new season. He won easily, and followed up impressively in the Newmarket Stakes. As a result he was strongly fancied to give his jockey, Charlie Smirke, a Derby success within a year of his return from a five year suspension, imposed for allegedly preventing an odds-on favourite, Welcome Gift, winning at Gatwick.

Smirke seized his opportunity with both hands, sending Windsor Lad past Tiberius with 2 furlongs to go and holding Easton by a length. The favourite, Colombo, was a fast-finishing third, prompting many observers to suggest that Rae Johnstone, his jockey, had ridden an ill-judged race. Marsh then prepared the colt for a tilt at the Eclipse in which he was beaten. Smirke got into a pocket in the straight and was beaten into third behind the four-year-old King Salmon with Umwidar second. Windsor Lad was never to be beaten again. After the Eclipse he was sold to the bookmaker, M.H. Benson for a reputed £50,000. For Mr Benson he won the Voltigeur and the St Leger, in which he equalled the record time of Coronach's 1926 victory.

As a four-year-old Windsor Lad proved beyond doubt that he was a superlative horse, winning the Burwell at Newmarket and the Coronation Cup. Put back to 7 furlongs he showed he had retained all his speed to win Ascot's Rous Memorial. Windsor Lad signed off in the Eclipse, where he beat Theft and the high-class Fair Trial. Windsor Lad was an above average Derby winner but his stud career was a failure. He was destroyed in 1943, after developing chronic sinus problems in 1938 which grew steadily worse.

Windsor Lad established Marcus Marsh's reputation. After returning from the war he moved to Newmarket to take over the Egerton House stables, where his father Richard had trained for two kings. He was to train another Derby winner, Tulyar, in 1952, also ridden by Charlie Smirke. One day in 1939, Marsh was reputedly so short of money that he expected the bailiffs to call at any moment. He rang his friend Randal Cramsie, a fellow trainer, exhorting him to remove his frigidaire, which was in those days a most modern appliance. Marsh, determined that the bailiffs would not secure his pride and joy, loaded the fridge into the boot of Cramsie's Bentley and transported it to Cramsie's residence nearby. Within days war was declared, and Marsh signed up for the RAF. After the war Cramsie rang Marsh one day to report the fridge was still working magnificently. Marsh, by then in funds, replied that Cramsie could keep it!

The Berkshire training grounds scored some notable achievements in the field of National Hunt racing during the years immediately preceding the Second World War. The 1938 National was won by the tiny stallion Battleship, owned by the wife of the American film star, Randolph Scott, and ridden by Bruce Hobbs – at seventeen years old the youngest rider ever to win. Battleship was trained at Rhonehurst in Upper Lambourn by the rider's father, Reg Hobbs. Reg Hobbs believed Battleship to be far too small at only 15 hands to cope with the huge Aintree fences. So little did he fancy his charge that he only accepted 1000–15 offered to him by a generous bookmaking friend 'in case he had to buy the champagne.' But the little American bred was more than equal to the task. In an exciting finish Bruce Hobbs, who was later to train a large string of flat horses at Newmarket, drove Battleship past the Dan Moore–ridden Royal Danieli in the closing stages of the race. Hobbs had ridden a perfectly timed race as Battleship had to be brought from behind in a finish, or he would down tools.

Further Liverpool success occurred in 1940, the last time the National was run for six years, because of the war. Bogskar, owned and trained by Lord Stalbridge at Pounds Farm, Eastbury, 2 miles south of Lambourn, thrilled a smallish crowd of many uniformed personnel, by beating the previous year's second, Macmoffat. Bogskar was ridden by Mervyn Jones, a nephew of Ivor Anthony, whose brother Owen had trained Lord Stalbridge's 1927 Cheltenham Gold Cup winner, Thrown In. Thrown In was ridden by Stalbridge's son Puck Grosvenor, who was killed in an accident in Australia soon after. Jones was sadly also to die two years after his Aintree triumph, during wartime service in the RAF. Lord Stalbridge

Ben Warner (left) and Ted Gwilt (right) – the owner and trainer of the 1937 Champion Hurdle winner, Free Fare. The flat jockey, Sam Wragg, is in the middle

was to have further wartime success in steeplechasing's top prizes. In 1945 his Red Rower was to win the Cheltenham Gold Cup, making amends for a 1942 defeat by the Lambourn horse Medoc II, trained by Reg Hobbs for Lord Sefton and ridden by Frenchie Nicholson. Red Rower was ridden by Davy (D.L.) Jones. Jones rode on the flat as well, and was to ride the second when the twelve-year-old Lester Piggott won his first ever race on The Chase at Haydock Park in 1948. Davy Jones rode work until a great age, dying recently at over ninety years of age. Lord Stalbridge's Eastbury triumphs were shared by Vernon Cross, who was the head lad at Pounds Farm. Cross was later to train on his own account at Atty Persse's famous stables, Chattis Hill near Stockbridge.

On the hurdling front, Ben Warner's Free Fare, trained at Saxon House, Upper Lambourn by Ted Gwilt, a Sussex parson's son, won the 1937 Champion Hurdle at Cheltenham, having been second the previous year. Free Fare had been a somewhat exasperating horse for his owner, who was one of the most formidable punters of the era. *The Sporting Life* of 1936, reporting on Free Fare's Manchester November Handicap win of that year, was moved to comment that Free Fare was 'something of an enigma. His owner were he less than phlegmatic would be either ecstatic or in despair. Twice he has swerved away the Manchester November Handicap, a race he won in a canter at the third time of asking when not so greatly fancied.' Free Fare was up to his old tricks in the 1937 Champion Hurdle as well. When produced by his rider, Georges Pellerin, after the second last, he veered sharply towards the steeplechase course. As a result, what would have been a facile victory was reduced to only a two-length advantage at the line.

In 1938 Free Fare was a hot favourite to regain the crown. However, ridden by Bruce Hobbs he fell at the second last when travelling easily. Our Hope, second to Free Fare the previous year, took advantage of the favourite's lapse to win under the famous amateur rider, Captain Perry Harding, to give Lambourn a second successive Champion Hurdle. Our Hope was owned and trained by Roderic Gubbins, a neighbour of Ted Gwilt's in the Berkshire village.

Compton in 1936 greeted a new arrival, when George Beeby moved from Leicestershire to take over Tom Cannon's old Hamilton House yard. Beeby, whose partnership with Lord Bicester was to be a major feature of National Hunt racing in the forties and fifties, was not long in making his mark from his new base. In 1939 he was to win his first Cheltenham

Gold Cup with Mrs Arthur Smith-Bingham's Brendan's Nephew ridden by George Owen. As well as Beeby, other famous names which were to feature prominently in post-war Berkshire racing, were starting their careers in the years preceding the Second World War. Arthur Budgett, who was to train and breed two Derby winners, trained briefly in Kirtlington before being called up. Fulke Walwyn, who had ridden Reynoldstown to victory at Aintree in 1936, was forced to give up a promising riding career after an horrendous fall in 1939. Walwyn chose Delamere House, Lambourn, where Windsor Lad was trained, to launch a training career which was to be one of the most successful that National Hunt racing has ever seen.

Berkshire stables achieved a notable catalogue of turf triumphs in the ninety years after Wild Dayrell's Derby. Many more were to come her way in the post-war era.

3
LAMBOURN – FLAT RACING 1945 TO THE PRESENT

As racing, run on a much reduced scale during the Second World War, sought to re-establish itself in the years immediately after the Armistice, new trainers, in many cases having lost precious years of their youth in the six years of war, joined those of the old guard, who, either through advancing age or being deemed medically unfit to fight, had gallantly kept their stables going in those difficult years of war.

Although Lambourn was to wait twenty–five long years after the end of war before celebrating another Classic success, some decent flat race horses were trained in the village before the golden years of the seventies. Fred Templeman's Radiotherapy flew the flag for the village in 1946, winning the prestigious mile race, the Sussex Stakes at Goodwood, after finishing third to Airborne in the Derby of that year. Atty Persse, the trainer of the 'Spotted Wonder', The Tetrarch, in those far off days before the First World War, concluded a distinguished training career, moving from his Chattis Hill, Stockbridge stables to Kingsdown, Upper Lambourn in 1945. Persse sent Durante from Kingsdown to win the Jubilee at Kempton two years in a row in the early fifties. In 1951 Persse also won the Royal Hunt Cup at Ascot with Val d'Assa and the King's Stand with Stephen Paul. In 1952 Stephen Paul took Doncaster's Portland and Queen of Sheba the Hunt Cup. Charlie Pratt, brother of Fred Pratt, who trained for many years at Waltham House, Upper Lambourn for Jimmy de Rothschild, ran a successful small stable at Uplands, where Fred Winter was to train. Pratt, who had been apprenticed to Fred Templeman's predecessor, John Hallick, had served as Harry Cottrill's travelling lad at Seven Barrows until 1931. Starting training soon after, his small yard won a number of important handicaps after the war. Pratt was tragically killed in a small plane accident returning home from Redcar in 1962, after landing his greatest win, the William Hill Gold Cup with Songedor.

Charlie Pratt was the last of his era to hold a licence in the village. His death in 1962 closed a distinguished chapter in Lambourn village's racing

Fred Pratt, who trained at Waltham House, Upper Lambourn for many years in the first half of the twentieth century. As a jockey Pratt won the 1895 1,000 Guineas on Galeottia

history: Captain Bell had died in 1949 and Harry Cottrill had left Seven Barrows in 1944, a year before old Fred Pratt had decided to call it a day at Waltham House. With Templeman to retire three years after Atty Persse, in 1956, there was much room in the village for new blood on the flat racing front.

Among the new post-war trainers in the village was Peter Nelson, who on his return from active service started training in the village in 1948 with only nine horses. An important early patron of Nelson's stable was the Maharanee of Baroda, who at one time held a third retainer on Sir Gordon Richards. The Maharanee was to provide Nelson with his first important winner, the fast two-year-old Whistler, who won the 1952 Coventry at Royal Ascot. Three years later Nelson was to score again at the Royal Meeting, winning the Queen Mary with Jack Olding's Weeber. Nelson was to build conclusively on these early successes, and by 1958 had assembled a string of forty-eight horses, a formidable amount for those days, at his Kingsdown yard where he had moved after Atty Persse's retirement. Firestreak, who won the 1960 City and Suburban, and Victorina who won the 1962 Stewards Cup, were distinguished inmates of the Nelson yard in the sixties. In the seventies Kingsdown, as we shall see, was to rise to even greater prominence.

Matt Feakes, the father-in-law of Jimmy Lindley, the ex-flat jockey and BBC commentator, trained at Rhonehurst, Reg Hobbs's old yard until the early sixties. He won the 1956 Jubilee at Kempton Park with Tudor Jinks for his long standing patron, Mr A.J. Tompsett, who also owned the fine miler of the early fifties, King's Bench. Also training in Upper Lambourn were two former champion jump jockeys, Bryan Marshall, who was at Berkeley House and Jack Dowdeswell at Neardown stables. Marshall was later to move to Compton and Dowdeswell to assist David Nugent with his small string of jumpers at Limes Farm further up the village. Peter Payne-Gallwey was at the Old Manor stables, and was to win the Stewards' Cup for two successive years in 1967 and 1968 with Sky Diver.

In Lambourn itself, Freddie Maxwell had moved in 1959 to the historic Lambourn House yard, after six years at Blewbury. In 1961 the Irishman had a wonderful year with the high-class stayer, Pandofell, who won the Queen's Prize, the Yorkshire and Doncaster Cups and the Ascot Gold Cup. Maxwell was to plunder the Gold Cup again in 1966 and 1967, with Lady Mairi Bury's Fighting Charlie. Maxwell had the fastest two-year-old filly of 1970 in Cawston's Pride, who won seven races that year. Maxwell was reputed to have coupled her in a Guineas double with a promising colt of his, Juggernaut, to win a fortune. Unfortunately the filly failed to train on, and Juggernaut proved not to be the required class. Maxwell, like many of his race, had a fund of stories, stretching back to the days he joined Aubrey Hastings's famous Wroughton stable in 1923. Maxwell recalled riding a horse, which was being transferred from Wroughton to Harry Cottrill's Seven Barrows yard, the whole way to the Shepherd's Rest public house below Foxhill – a long distance from Wroughton. After passing the horse to Cottrill's lad, Maxwell had to walk the whole way back to Wroughton again. Needless to say these were the days before the horsebox became commonplace. Maxwell retired in 1977, and continued to live in Lambourn until his recent death.

Another great character training in the village at the time was Sandy Carlos-Clarke, who built much of the Hill House establishment in the Folly Road with his own fair hand. Carlos-Clarke, who had originally come to Lambourn to assist his then brother-in-law, Fulke Walwyn, had a fair bit of success in the fifties and early sixties with horses named after various wartime Commando units: No. 4 Commando was a notable example. The captain had served gallantly in such units himself, but was reputedly so nervous when he had a fancied runner that he used to shut himself in the Gentlemens' and pull the chain at regular intervals to drown the commentator. He would then emerge without the faintest idea whether his charge had been successful. Carlos-Clarke sold the Hill House establishment to Paul Cole a few years after his retirement, and lives in Lambourn to this day.

Bob Read, who owned the famous Windmill Gallops, trained at Bourne House on the outskirts of the village. Read, who won the Steward's Cup in 1964 with Dunme, used to gallop his two-year-olds up a little lane in the spring of the year to 'buck' their shins. He claimed this practice prevented them from suffering from sore shins when the firm summer ground arrived.

At South Bank, where Barry Hills now trains, Keith Piggott ran a successful mixed stable. His career as a trainer was to reach its zenith when he won the National of 1963 with Ayala. Although Keith Piggott's flat string may not have consisted of animals of the highest class, a human star was to emerge in 1948 from the stable set on the hill above the Eastbury road.

On 18 August, 1948, a minor selling race, the Wigan Selling Plate at Haydock Park, was to provide the first ever winner for one of the most enduring legends of the turf: Keith Piggott's tiny young son, Lester, was to drive The Chase to victory at the tender age of twelve years old. In 1950 the young fourteen-year-old was fully established as one of the country's top light-weight jockeys: combining race riding with his schooling at King Alfred's in Wantage, Lester rode the winners of fifty-two races from 404 mounts. The young jockey had quickly attracted the attention of the leading trainers, who recognized his incredible natural ability and his relentless will to win.

It is well known that the will to win, characteristic of Piggott's riding to this day, incurred the wrath of the stewards in those early years. In 1950 Piggott was suspended for the remainder of the season after an incident in Newbury that October. Worse was to follow. In 1954, at the Royal Ascot meeting after his first Derby triumph on Never Say Die, Piggott was deemed to have ridden that same horse dangerously, without regard to the safety of other jockeys. His licence was withdrawn and the stewards let it be known that they would not countenance any application for its renewal for a further six months, during which time he would have to serve his apprenticeship with a trainer other than his father. This decision was to sever the great jockey's connection with Lambourn. Immediately he was dispatched to the powerful Newmarket stable of Jack

Humble Duty, the 1970 1,000 Guineas winner and Lester Piggott

Jarvis, who at the time retained Piggott's cousin, Bill Rickaby, as first jockey. In 1955 Piggott resumed his career, taking over from the retiring Gordon Richards as first jockey to the élite stable of Noel Murless in Newmarket. The rest is history.

Although the harsh decision of the stewards in Portman Square deprived Keith Piggott of the responsibility for his son's career, his early tutelage on the Lambourn downs set in motion and ironed out the edges of the greatest riding talent this country has ever seen. If anybody was ever bred to be a jockey it was Lester Piggott. His father Keith had been a distinguished steeplechase jockey before training. Keith Piggott's father, Ernie, himself a great jump jockey, had married the daughter of Tom Cannon of Danebury, himself a champion flat rider and father of Mornington and Kempton Cannon, fine jockeys themselves. Tom Cannon was John Day's son-in-law. Piggott on his father's side was therefore a direct descendant of old John Barham Day. His mother, Iris, was a daughter of Frederick Rickaby, who was attached to old Mat Dawson's Newmarket stable and rode three Classic winners in the 1890s. Iris Piggott's father Fred was the grandson of the Rickaby who trained Berkshire's first Derby winner, Wild Dayrell in 1855. His son, Frederick Lester Rickaby, rode five Classic winners, including Charles Morton's fine filly, Jest, before being killed in the First World War. He was the father of Bill Rickaby, the rider of Sweet Solera and Busted. His other son, Fred, trained in South Africa with distinction for many years.

At Seven Barrows Bill Payne, who had taken out a lease on the establishment from Captain Ronnie Bennett of Kingstone Warren in 1947, three years after Harry Cottrill's departure, had noticed the emerging talent of the young Lester Piggott. In 1952, he provided the young apprentice with an important early big race success when the enigmatic Zucchero, who had ruined his chance in the 1951 Derby by virtually refusing to start, won the Princess of Wales at Newmarket. The next year Piggott and Zucchero won Epsom's Coronation Cup, beating the good stayer Wilwyn, and providing Payne with his biggest success at Seven Barrows since winning the 1950 King's Stand with Tangle.

Payne's fortunes, however, did not improve. Finding the huge rent and overheads of the large establishment too great, he retired in 1955. His son, Bill, trained a small string in Eastbury with success for many years and is the father of the current Newmarket trainer Pip Payne. In 1958 the lease was taken on by David Hastings. In 1961, on the death of the Countess of Craven, the huge Craven estates were broken up. Seven Barrows was put on the market, and the Kingstone Warren trainer Derrick Candy bought both properties to secure the freehold on his Kingstone Warren stable, also part of the same lot. He sublet Seven Barrows to Hastings, who experienced similar problems to his predecessor, and moved to Weathercock House, Upper Lambourn. Candy decided to sell the famous Seven Barrows yard.

Peter Walwyn, a cousin of Fulke Walwyn, had moved to the Windsor House yard in the village in 1960, on the retirement of Syd Mercer, who trained Trelawny to win the Chester Cup. Trelawny had broken down later in the Goodwood Stakes. The vets recommended that he should be destroyed but Mercer, having none of it, nursed the old horse back to health. He was to win many long distance races for years after, under the care of Jack Colling and George Todd. Walwyn, who had previously worked for Geoffrey Brooke at Newmarket before holding the licence for his cousin, Helen Johnson-Houghton, at Blewbury, took on Mercer's head lad, Ray Laing. Soon the young trainer was attracting racing's attention and the size of his string was increasing. In the spring of 1964 Derrick Candy's wife Cerise meeting Walwyn's string at exercise, shouted across to the thirty-year-old trainer: 'Would you like to buy Seven Barrows?' By March 1965 Walwyn, having raised the necessary finance, moved his stable to the historic establishment where Kettledrum had galloped before the 1861 Derby. The era of the huge flat race stable, so prevalent in the modern day, was soon to come to this neck of Berkshire.

Walwyn soon found a class horse to attract attention to his new stable. In his first year at Seven Barrows Mabel, bred on the Welsh borders by G.P. Williams, finished third in the 1,000 Guineas and second in the Oaks. Most notably she won the prestigious Yorkshire Oaks. Walwyn's handling of Mabel established her trainer's reputation as a fine handler of fillies. His early years at Seven Barrows are memorable for the number of high quality fillies that passed through his hands. 1969 produced two

Peter Walwyn directing operations on the gallops

more. Frontier Goddess won the Yorkshire Oaks and finished second in the Epsom equivalent. Lucyrowe won the Coronation at Royal Ascot and the Nassau at Goodwood, having been an unlucky loser in the Guineas, when interfered with at a vital stage. In the two-year-old department, Jean, Lady Ashcombe's Humble Duty carried all before her – winning the Cheveley Park at Newmarket to confirm she was the best filly of her age. These successes did much to attract prominent owner breeders to Walwyn's stable. Far more numerous than in the modern day, these owners were to be the basis for many of the trainer's triumphs in the ensuing years.

Humble Duty proved herself the top miler of her generation, providing Lambourn with a first Classic winner since the war, when winning the 1,000 Guineas in the hands of Lester Piggott, Walwyn's stable jockey, Duncan Keith, having to forfeit the ride due to illness. But ill luck plagued Walwyn's representatives in the Epsom Classics in the early Seven Barrows years; another Oaks runner-up was Mrs Dermot McCalmont's State Pension in 1970. In the colt department Shoemaker and Linden Tree both finished second in the Derbys of 1969 and 1970 respectively.

Pat Eddery and Frank Morby – first and second jockeys to Peter Walwyn's Seven Barrows stable in the 1970s

Worse luck occurred in Royal Ascot's feature, the Gold Cup. In 1971 Rock Roi, after scoring in facile fashion, was disqualified after traces of a painkiller, used some time before, were found in the horse's urine. Unbelievably, Rock Roi won again in 1972, only to lose the race in the stewards' room. The stewards deemed the unlucky stayer to have interfered with the neck second, Erimo Hawk, ridden by the young Pat Eddery who was later to figure in many Seven Barrows successes.

Duncan Keith, Walwyn's stable jockey, retired during 1972 as he was unable to cope with increasing weight trouble. Walwyn made a decision which he was never to regret, choosing the twenty-year-old Pat Eddery as Keith's successor. Eddery vindicated the trainer's decision by winning the Dewhurst on Dick Poole's Lunchtime in the autumn of that year. Although Lunchtime proved a disappointment in his three-year-old career the new partnership had a wonderful year: Eddery finishing top jockey at Royal Ascot, courtesy of several Walwyn winners, including the subsequent Middle Park victor, Habat. In 1974 Walwyn laid the Epsom bogey to rest when Eddery steered Louis Freedman's Polygamy to victory in the Oaks. Walwyn was leading trainer for the first time that year, winning ninety-six races, worth £206,783.

Walwyn, capitalizing on his success on the racecourse, developed the Seven Barrows establishment during the late sixties and seventies to rival any of its counterparts. A huge indoor school was built to ensure the string was never held up in the hard winter months, and an all-weather gallop was laid out on the Faringdon Road gallop, one of the first of its kind in the area. Walwyn doubled the horse capacity of his yard by constructing two barns in the American style. He also constructed canters in the paddocks close to his yard to ensure his horses had a change of scenery from the stiff straight Faringdon Road gallops on the downs. By 1974 the Seven Barrows establishment was the most modern private establishment of its kind in the country, well capable of housing the hundred and more thoroughbreds that Walwyn had to train. These years saw Lambourn's first encounter with the huge flat strings, which were to be a feature of the village's development as a major flat racing centre. Walwyn set this process in motion with his success in the seventies, a significant decade in the village's history.

In 1974, a flashy chestnut colt by Great Nephew was proving quite a handful to ride. Full of the joys of youth, Grundy was not a popular morning mount at Seven Barrows, regularly depositing his jockeys on the floor. Matt McCormack, who had recently arrived at the stable as a head lad from Newmarket, rode him out one day and soon had established a rapport with the difficult two-year-old, which was to last for the whole of the horse's racing career. In July 1974 Grundy was showing Walwyn plenty of talent. The Granville Stakes at Ascot, an event for unraced colts on King George day, was chosen for the chestnut's racecourse debut. Ridden by Eddery, he scored with the minimum of fuss from his stable companion No Alimony. Victory in the Dewhurst over the Middle Park winner Steel Heart ensured Grundy went into winter quarters with good prospects of further Classic success for Walwyn's stable.

During the winter Grundy did well, maturing into a splendid specimen. In March disaster struck. Grundy, his customary boisterous self, leapt forward towards his stable companion Corby in the indoor school one morning. Corby retaliated, kicking Grundy extremely hard in the head above the temple. Although the tough colt recovered quickly, Walwyn lost some vital days in his Guineas preparation. Grundy went to his preliminary race, the Greenham, short of work. Heavy ground that day did not help. He was beaten by the superfit Mark Anthony by two lengths, the Newmarket trained colt relishing the testing conditions. In the Guineas Grundy, stripping considerably fitter, ran a great race to be beaten half a length by Bolkonski. Two weeks later he scored comfortably in the Irish equivalent at the Curragh. Subsequent work with his galloping companions saw Walwyn a confident man at Epsom in June.

Grundy beating the French filly Nobiliary in the 1975 Derby

Grundy at 5–1 second favourite won the Derby by three lengths from the filly Nobiliary to establish himself as the best staying three-year-old of the year. A decisive victory in the Irish Derby followed. By July the racing world waited with bated breath for the result of Grundy's greatest test, his first encounter against the best of the older generation in the King George VI and Queen Elizabeth at Ascot. Grundy's duel with the four-year-old Bustino up the Ascot straight will never be forgotten. After a blistering early pace set by Bustino's two pacemakers, Grundy, repeatedly answering Eddery's calls for more, finally beat Bustino by half a length, with the high class filly Dahlia five lengths away in third. Returning to the unsaddling enclosure to rousing cheers, the gallant chestnut looked exhausted. It transpired that Grundy had given his all that July afternoon: he only ran once again, in that graveyard for Classic horses, the Benson and Hedges at York. A tired horse, he finished fourth to Dahlia whom he had easily defeated at Ascot.

There is little doubt that Grundy was the best Classic winner ever trained in Lambourn. His defeat of the best older horse of 1975, Bustino, proved his class conclusively. Strangely, like many good horses he worked unimpressively at home when at the peak of condition. Taken by Walwyn to work on Henry Candy's famous White Horse Hill before his King George triumph, he refused to exert himself, finishing behind some infinitely inferior galloping companions. Eddery who rode him in the gallop was not worried, reporting to the trainer the colt had become lazy. The jockey was subsequently proved more than correct in his assessment. It is a fact that a lazy horse who reserves his best for the racecourse will often last longer at his peak on the stiff Berkshire downs.

The late seventies brought further success to Seven Barrows with Vitiges winning the 1976 Champion Stakes, the top sprinter Record Token taking the Vernons at Haydock, and the miler Free State scoring in the Waterford Crystal at Goodwood. New owners joined the stable, among them the art dealer Daniel Wildenstein, who moved all his horses from France to Walwyn in the spring of 1978. Among Wildenstein's string to arrive from Chantilly were the high-class stayer Buckskin and the top-class performer, Crow. Although Walwyn won the Cadran with Buckskin, the horse had poor feet and proved difficult to train, losing vital days exercise on several occasions. His defeat in the Ascot Gold Cup of 1978 infuriated Wildenstein who blamed Eddery's riding, although due to his many enforced lay-offs Buckskin had in fact blown up close to home. Walwyn with characteristic loyalty, refused to replace Eddery, and Wildenstein sent his horses to the Newmarket yard of Henry Cecil. In June, Walwyn took Epsom's Coronation Cup with Crow. This was one of the trainer's most formidable achievements. Realizing quickly that Crow did not like the regimentation of work with the string, he trained the light-framed, clean-winded horse almost exclusively in the paddocks around his house, sweetening up the old campaigner to such a degree that he regained his old form to score comfortably at Epsom.

A long virus attack, similar to that which affected Dick Hern's stable in the 1960s, was responsible for Walwyn losing another class animal, the Greek shipping magnate Stavros Niarchos's Nureyev. Sent to the French yard of Francois Boutin after contracting the disease, the subsequently disqualified Guineas winner was unraced when he left Seven Barrows. It is not widely known that Nureyev was showing tremendous speed in early work in the summer of 1979. Walwyn, recognizing the tremendous talent of the horse, decided to give Nureyev more time to mature. If Walwyn had not had the best interests of the young Northern Dancer colt at heart, there is no doubt he would have triumphed with ease at Royal Ascot. Niarchos, an impatient owner, might well have left the little horse at Seven Barrows.

In 1992 it was announced that Walwyn would change stables with Nick Henderson, thus returning to the yard at Windsor House where he had started nearly thirty years before. With fewer horses than in the golden years of the seventies, Walwyn could no longer run the huge establishment economically. With his departure the most successful era of the famous old stables was to close. For the first time for 150 years a jumping string would be resident at Garrett Moore's old yard.

Some years ago an owner rang Walwyn saying he wished to sell a promising horse. He needed the money to re-tar the lengthy drive on his estate. Walwyn, furious when the horse won some decent prizes during the following year, telephoned the owner, telling him he could have tarred the interior of his house as well, if he had kept his horse.

While Seven Barrows thrived in the seventies, the village of Lambourn also experienced long overdue Classic success. In early 1974, Peter Nelson had a promising three-year-old colt at his Kingsdown stable named Snow Knight. Bought cheaply as a yearling by Nelson's wife, Mac, he had shown decent, if not top-class, form as a two-year-old being narrowly beaten in Doncaster's Champagne Stakes. His early three-year-old career appeared to show him just below the highest class, being placed behind Bustino in the Sandown and Lingfield Derby trials. Starting at 50–1 at Epsom, he led the whole way under an inspired ride from Brian Taylor to score comfortably, producing one of the biggest post-war Derby shocks. Snow Knight never showed such form in England again, being beaten in his next five races. After being exported to Canada in the autumn he found top-class form again on the American circuit, winning amongst other good races the Man O'War Stakes. The hard ground prevalent at Epsom in the long hard summer of 1974 may have been responsible for some of Snow Knight's rivals running below form. Nevertheless his Derby was justifiable reward for Peter Nelson, who had during a long career in Lambourn run a consistently successful flat stable. Before his retirement in 1976 after nearly thirty years with a licence, Nelson had charge of the high-class sprinter Bay Express, who won the 1974 King's Stand and the 1975 Nunthorpe, now known as the William Hill Sprint Championship.

In 1969 Barry Hills, with funds from a formidable coup on John

Barry Hills, the Lambourn trainer

Oxley's Frankincense in the Lincoln of the previous year, bought Keith Piggott's South Bank stable and commenced his training career. Hills, whose father had been Tom Rimell's travelling lad, had been in racing all his life. As Oxley's travelling lad, he had always appeared to his colleagues as likely to go far. More often than not he would arrive at the racecourse in some expensive automobile, while his counterparts travelled in the less comfortable confines of the horsebox. After two years, Hills had won his first pattern race with Lord Porchester's Disguise. In 1972 he had two three-year-old colts of the highest class in his Lambourn yard, Rheingold and Our Mirage.

Rheingold's victory in the Dante, and Our Mirage's success in the Dee stakes at Chester, ensured that the South Bank stable had two live prospects for the Derby in June. Both representatives were to acquit themselves with credit. Rheingold, ridden by Hill's stable jockey Ernie Johnson, going under by a short head to the Piggott-ridden Roberto with Our Mirage finishing a creditable fourth. Many observers believe that Piggott's finish on Roberto was the most powerful the great jockey ever rode. Rheingold's near miss in 1972 was to prove a portent. Hills was to experience many more in his quest to win the two Epsom Classics.

Hawaiian Sound was to look like winning under the American champion Bill Shoemaker, in 1978, until Shirley Heights passed him close home. In 1988 and 1990 Hills was to finish second with Glacial Storm and Blue Stag. If the Derby has proved an elusive race for the South Bank trainer, so has the Oaks. Dibidale on subsequent form appeared to have been robbed of victory by a slipping saddle in 1974. In 1976 Hills saddled the Oaks favourite Durtal, only to see her throw Piggott on the canter to the post and crash into the rails, sustaining an injury that necessitated her withdrawal. In 1982, Hills saddled Slightly Dangerous and Last Feather to finish second and third to Time Charter. The two Epsom Classics still elude him to this day.

The splendid performances of Rheingold and Our Mirage saw the strength of Hills's string rise rapidly. In 1973 he had assembled 104 horses under his care. Rapid building programmes were undertaken at South Bank, and the small yard soon grew and grew, boxes being erected in every available space. Overflow yards, such as Fred Templeman's old stable at Meridian, were leased by Hills to cater for his ever expanding string. Rheingold's victory in the 1973 Arc de Triomphe under Lester Piggott gave Hills international recognition. His string maintains a huge proportion of foreign owners to this day.

In 1978 Hills won his first domestic Classic with the filly Enstone Spark, owned by the Canadian Dick Bonnycastle. Trained as a two-year-old by Richard Hannon, Enstone Spark was sold in the winter of her two-year-old career, as her previous owner's rapidly declining sight prevented him from seeing her run. Starting at 35-1 under Ernie Johnson, she won the 1,000 Guineas at Newmarket on her first outing of the season. In 1979 Hills won the 2,000 with Tony Shead's Tap on Wood, to provide the recently arrived young American Steve Cauthen with his first British Classic. The 1980s provided Hills with many other important successes. The filly Cormorant Wood, improving with age, landed the Champion Stakes and the Benson and Hedges, and Gildoran triumphed for two consecutive years in the Ascot Gold Cup.

In 1987 Barry Hills moved to the Manton stables of one of his oldest patrons, Robert Sangster, and handed over South Bank to his son John. His second yard at Bourne House was sold to Nick Henderson and it appeared that Lambourn had lost his large string for ever more. By 1990 Hills had failed to raise the necessary finance to buy the Manton showpiece, and Sangster took Manton off the market. Hills was forced to move his huge string back to Lambourn. His son John moved to Hill House stables, and Hills leased John Francome's newly constructed stable on Sheepdrove as a second yard to South Bank. The move back to Lambourn saw Hills maintain his usual consistency, winning in 1991 six pattern races, including the Goodwood Mile with Bold Russian.

The rapid rise of Barry Hills's fortunes in the early seventies provides one of racing's most durable success stories. Hills is the first to admit that sometimes in the early days he did not know where he was going to find the money for next week's wages. The consistency of Hills in producing class horses year in year out is a notable feature of the trainer's record. At time of writing he has won over a hundred British pattern races, an achievement only equalled by three current trainers, Dick Hern, Henry Cecil and Michael Stoute. The majority have been trained at Lambourn. In the late seventies Hills purchased the northern side of the Faringdon Road gallops, having previously used Peter Walwyn's facilities. Although a fair distance from South Bank the trainer has always believed this to be a bonus, ensuring his string has a healthy appetite on their return home. Hills, who cuts a dapper figure with his immaculate suits on the racecourse, once said he would retire at fifty. Now he claims he cannot afford to. The large cigar which is his trademark will surely be seen in the enclosures of the major racecourses for many years to come.

Although the huge strings of Hills and Walwyn attracted most of the publicity in those years, there is no doubt the village of Lambourn thrived as a result of their continuous success. Although space precludes the mention of many, some notable characters trained in the village at the time. Doug Marks is one of the oldest residents. Marks who rode Godiva to win the 1,000 Guineas and Oaks in 1940 as a seventeen-year-old, came to Lambourn in 1965 after training at the now defunct Ascot Cottage stables at Winkfield. Having sold the Uplands stable to Fred Winter he moved to Waltham House, where Fred Pratt had trained for many years. In the sixties Marks trained several top sprinters, usually bought from other yards and rejuvenated by the shrewd trainer. Fireside Chat and Shiny Tenth were notable examples. Marks is possessed of a notable sense of humour. One day he instructed his string to walk around a tree on Mandown and await his arrival. As the lads walked round the tree for what seemed an eternity, their language became bluer and bluer, as they described the absent trainer with every expletive under the sun. Finally they were amazed to see their missing boss climb down from the branches, delighting in their embarrassment as he had heard every one of their insults. In the early eighties Marks sold most of his Lethornes yard to Michael Blanshard. He now trains only a small number of horses, devoting most of his time to his first love, golf.

Another resident of Upper Lambourn during the sixties was Ben Leigh, who bought the Neardown establishment on Jack Dowdeswell's retirement. Leigh, who trained the good two-year-old Brer Rabbit, believed in giving his string some strenuous gallops on the downs. One day a week he used to send them on a trot to recover from their exertions of the previous day's work. His staff, soon realizing that the trainer preferred to have a lie-in on this particular morning, used to walk down the drive to the road and then walk back up the grass verge to the yard to muffle the sound of the hooves. Leigh, by then fast asleep again, believed them to be safely out on the long trot he had ordered, when in fact his staff were taking an early breakfast in the more comfortable confines of his tack room.

Dave Hanley moved to Lambourn in 1966 from Epsom. In 1969 he sent Big Hat from his Delamere stables to win York's Ebor Handicap. One year, Hanley had a decent dark horse in his stable named Great Ball, who had been showing up well on the gallops. Hanley, realizing his horse had a bit of class, landed some big bets on him in a maiden in the Midlands. Returning home that night after much celebration, he decided for safety's sake to bury his new-found wealth in the field opposite his house. The next morning strings walking to exercise on the Baydon Road were amazed to see the trainer frantically retrieving wads of notes in a miraculous nature from the virgin soil, in the company of a distinguished local vet.

Lambourn's remaining Classic success of the seventies fell to one of the smaller training establishments. Duncan Sasse, who had started his career in meteoric fashion by winning the Eclipse with Coup de Feu in his first season's training of 1974, received a new inmate at his Frenchmans stables in Upper Lambourn in the autumn of 1977. His father, Tim, who had owned a proportion of Rheingold, had purchased a controlling interest in the disqualified Horris Hill winner Roland Gardens. Moving the horse immediately from Robert Armstrong's Newmarket stable, he sent it to his son Duncan. Roland Gardens went to Newmarket a 28–1 chance, having previously scored in the Blue Riband at Epsom. He ran on strongly to take the 1978 2,000 Guineas in the hands of the veteran jockey Frank Durr, beating Remainder Man. Sadly Roland Gardens never regained his form again and was exported to South Africa at the end of his four-year-old career. His young trainer's sole Classic victory did not provide the necessary momentum to his career. In 1985 Sasse sold his stables to David Murray-Smith and moved to sunnier climes in Italy. In 1992 he returned to try his luck with a small string, based just outside Newmarket.

Paul Cole, who had started with just three horses in 1968, had by shrewd placings of the moderate horses in his care increased the size of his Hill House stable to sixty inmates by the start of the 1973 season. In 1977 Cole won the Robert Papin at Deauville with John de Coombe, to supplement two big sprint handicap victories in the Wokingham and Stewards Cup with the fast filly Calibina. In 1979 the good stayer Crimson Beau won the Prince of Wales, and in 1980 Queen's Pride gave Cole a second Wokingham. The increased patronage of the Saudi owner, Fahd Salman, saw the quality of Cole's string increase and with the Saudi prince's backing, Cole looked for larger premises, feeling his large string was beginning to create congestion on the public facilities in Lambourn. In 1985 protracted negotiations were completed, and Cole's one hundred horse string moved to the famous stable at Whatcombe, a few miles across Berkshire. Lambourn, it will be seen, was to lose two Classic winners as a result of Cole's important decision.

The rise in quality of Paul Cole's string during those last years in Lambourn was in stark contrast to the decline in quantity that many of his Lambourn neighbours were to suffer as the recession of the late eighties and nineties hit the luxury sport of racing. Several yards which had enjoyed significant success in the boom years of the early eighties were to close. Decreasing patronage, as English owners left the sport in droves, unpaid training bills and ever escalating interest charges were to persuade Nick Vigors, Mark Smyly, Kim Brassey and Merrick Francis to hand in their licences and call it a day. Charlie Nelson, who had won £100,000 in stakes in 1983, due in the main to the exploits of the Middle Park winner Creag-an-Sgor, and the good filly Mahogany, has a much depleted string. John Hills and Charles Elsey are sons of famous fathers seeking to establish themselves in these difficult times. Mike Channon, the former England footballer, is another to achieve much in his short time in Fulke Walwyn's old second yard in Upper Lambourn. William Muir, son of the former owner of the Fawley Stud, is assembling a good-sized string in the famous old Delamere stables on the Folly Road. Michael Blanshard won the 1992 Chester Cup with Welshman, and is now experiencing a deserved resurgence of his fortunes.

Kingwood stables – Dick Hern's new stable at Lambourn

Sadly, the big races that inevitably attract the greatest media publicity seem to fall with increasing regularity into the hands of the Arab princes, who dominate the sport in the present day. Dick Hern, from his lavish newly constructed stable on the hill at Kingwood, Mark Smyly's old establishment, has Hamdan al Maktoum as his principal patron. Peter Walwyn's stable is increasingly dominated by the same man. Barry Hills also enjoys significant Arab patronage. It is a fair bet that Lambourn's next class flat horse will emanate from one of these sources. It is pertinent to note that it is Arab money which built the new stable and facilities at Kingwood. In these hard times it is important for the village of Lambourn that the Arabs continue to invest in and patronize the sport. Without them Lambourn's position as a major flat race centre would diminish to a dangerously low level. The banks see racing as a dangerous investment in these times of recession, while the lowering of property values has made many stables depreciating assets. Many Lambourn yards are on the market with no buyers on the horizon. The famous training centre is presently experiencing hard times, perhaps the hardest of its long and distinguished history.

4
THE REST OF BERKSHIRE – FLAT RACING 1945 TO THE PRESENT

As Lambourn produced some notable post-war triumphs in the field of flat racing, her fellow Berkshire stables further east were not left in her wake. Whatcombe saw the start of Michael Beary's training career in 1951. Beary knew Whatcombe well, as the Aga Khan's retained jockey in the days when the Aga patronized Dick Dawson's stable. The arrival of the good two-year-old Ki Ming, transferred from Beary's brother John's East Hendred stable in the spring of 1951, was to prove an unexpected bonus for the new trainer. Ki Ming moved to Whatcombe as a positive dope test on John Beary's La Joyeuse in October 1950 resulted in the East Hendred trainer having his licence withdrawn. In those days, warning off was the harsh penalty for this offence. There is no doubt that John Beary was greatly involved in Ki Ming's 2,000 Guineas preparation, but it was his brother Michael who received the accolades when Scobie Breasley drove the huge sprint-bred colt to beat a substandard field at Newmarket. Although he started favourite for the Derby, Ki Ming ran out of stamina, finishing unplaced behind Arctic Prince. Reverting to shorter distances, Ki Ming won Ascot's Diadem later in the year. Beary, receiving little patronage despite his first season Classic win, returned to race riding in 1953, having run into financial problems early in his brief training career.

In 1951 Arthur Budgett, who had trained Commissar to land a huge coup in the Lincoln of 1948, moved from Nelson House, East Ilsley to Whatcombe. Budgett had begun training at Kirtlington, his Oxfordshire home, for a brief period before the outbreak of war. At Kirtlington Budgett still ran the Park Farm Stud, an establishment which was to provide the famous stables with some animals of the highest class in the ensuing years. In 1961 Budgett purchased a filly foal by Hornbeam from the breeder, Major Lionel Holliday, for 1,000 gns at the December Sales. Reoffered as a yearling she failed to reach a 5,000 gns reserve price. Subsequently she entered Budgett's stable to earn her keep, the trainer leasing her for the duration of her racing career to two patrons of his stable, Sir Jeffrey Darell and Miss Betty Rigden.

The filly foal, named Windmill Girl, was to prove a race mare of the highest class. In the Oaks of 1964 she made up a phenomenal amount of ground in the straight to finish second to Homeward Bound, beaten by only two lengths, despite losing ground by hanging continuously towards the stand rail. Sent to Royal Ascot, she made amends by winning the Ribblesdale Stakes. Later she ran an excellent race to finish third in the Irish Oaks. Retired to stud, she was covered by Major Holiday's Leger winner, Hethersett, and in 1966 produced a bay colt. Like his mother before him, fortunately for Budgett he failed to reach a 5,000 gns reserve at the Newmarket yearling sales and was sent into training at Whatcombe in the winter. Budgett kept a half share himself and sold the remaining quarters to Mrs Diana Carnegie and Horace Renshaw.

The bay colt, named Blakeney, was given time to mature. At Ascot in September he had his first outing, running with promise for an animal with a staying pedigree, to finish fourth to the Noel Murless-trained Caliban. Sent to Newmarket he won the Houghton Stakes from a big field, ridden by Ernie Johnson. After the race Arthur Budgett promised Johnson the ride at Epsom if Blakeney should prove up to Derby class. The colt was retired for the season after Newmarket. Blakeney took some time to come to himself next spring. It was not until mid-May that he had his first outing in the Lingfield Derby trial. Ridden by Geoff Lewis, he appeared to be given plenty to do and was just beaten by The Elk, the previous year's Observer Gold Cup winner. Lewis reported that the colt would have won if he had not experienced interference. He pleaded with Budgett to ride the horse at Epsom and was most disappointed to learn that Johnson had been promised the ride.

At Epsom, Johnson settled Blakeney in the middle of the field until Tattenham Corner. Making his effort down the rail, he shot through on the inside of the subsequent second Shoemaker inside the final furlong, to win by a fairly comfortable length. Blakeney's victory brought Whatcombe its first Derby since Dawson's day. Arthur Budgett had achieved a formidable first. He had bred, owned and trained a Derby winner. The rest of Blakeney's three-year-old career was somewhat disappointing. He was fourth in the Irish Derby to Prince Regent, whom he had beaten at Epsom. After finishing fifth in the St Leger, he ran ninth in the Arc de Triomphe and was retired for the season.

His connections decided sportingly to campaign him as a four-year-old, a decision that many modern-day owners would not have dared make. Although he won the Ormonde at Chester in May, he was not to win again. The last Derby winner to run in the Ascot Gold Cup, he ran a gutsy race to finish a three-quarter-length second to the Rosemary Lomax-trained Precipice Wood. Brought back in distance, Nijinsky had too much class for him in the King George VI, Blakeney being beaten by two lengths. Finally he made his second attempt at the Arc, finishing fifth to Sassafras and Nijinsky. Blakeney was then retired to stud. He had the distinction of siring a Classic winner from his very first crop, when Juliette Marny won the Oaks of 1975.

In the same year that Blakeney won the Derby, Budgett sent his mother Windmill Girl to another St Leger winner, Ragusa. The result of this mating was a chestnut colt named Morston. Backward like his brother Blakeney, he never ran at two. His first appearance was in a minor maiden race, the Godstone Plate at Lingfield Park in May. Morston, ridden by Frank Durr, ran out a comfortable winner that day and Budgett, with some reservation due to the horse's inexperience, decided to let Morston take his chance at Epsom, believing the race to be of a slightly substandard nature. Budgett's stable jockey at the time Geoff Baxter, preferred to ride the more fancied Whatcombe entrant, Projector. With Frank Durr unavailable, Budgett booked the leading northern jockey Edward Hide for Morston. Hide had never sat astride Morston before Derby day. Starting at 25–1 he took the lead a furlong out and held off Cavo Doro ridden by his breeder Lester Piggott to win by half a length. Lightning had struck twice: Windmill Girl had bred a second Derby winner. Sadly both Windmill Girl and Morston's sire Ragusa had died before the Derby. Budgett had owned, trained and bred his second Derby winner in four years, an achievement unlikely to be ever matched. The difference was that, unlike Blakeney, he owned Morston outright! Morston was never able to show how good a Derby winner he was. He sustained a leg injury later in training and never ran again.

Budgett's head lad at Whatcombe, Tom Dowdeswell, brother of the champion jump jockey Jack, had, as a result of Morston's Derby victory, incredibly been associated with four Derby winners in his long career. He had looked after Windsor Lad in Lambourn for Marcus Marsh and travelled Tulyar to Epsom for the same trainer when he had moved after the war to Newmarket. Although the two Derby victories were the highlight of Budgett's career at Whatcombe, he trained a number of other top-class

Paul Cole's horses before the start of a gallop on Woolley Down

animals in his twenty-four years there.

In 1963 Budgett won the Cornwallis Stakes at Ascot for Mrs Renshaw, wife of Blakeney's part owner with the two-year-old Derring Do. After a good three-year-old year, Derring-Do blossomed at four, winning the Queen Elizabeth Stakes at Ascot, proving himself one of the country's leading milers. Derring-Do was subsequently to sire the fastest horse Budgett ever trained, Huntercombe. Huntercombe was the fastest two-year-old of 1969, winning the Middle Park, the July Stakes and the Cornwallis. Unlike many precocious two-year-olds, Huntercombe carried all before him in the sprinting field at three, winning the July Cup and the Nunthorpe. He showed such blistering speed on the Woolley gallops that horses had to be jumped in at intervals in his work to give him some company. In the early seventies Budgett trained the high-class stayer Random Shot, who won the Ascot Gold Cup by default after Rock Roi's positive dope test. Budgett always had a penchant for laying a horse out for the big handicaps, no doubt fuelled by his early success with Commissar. Hook Money, who won the 1955 Ayr Gold Cup was a notable example; as was that great old campaigner of the early seventies, Petty Officer, who loved plundering the big handicaps that Redcar put on in those days.

In 1974 Budgett handed over the majority of his string to his longtime assistant James Bethell, retaining just ten horses in a small yard he had constructed at Whatcombe specifically for this purpose. Among the ten was the high-class miler, Dominion, who finished third in the 1975 2,000 Guineas and subsequently has proved to be a high-class stallion. Budgett declined to renew his licence again, and retired to Kirtlington to concentrate on the stud where he had bred Morston and Blakeney. He was made a member of the Jockey Club in 1977.

At the end of 1977 James Bethell moved to new quarters at Whitsbury in Hampshire, where Sir Gordon Richards had trained Reform. The famous yard at Whatcombe was to lie dormant, unused for the next seven years. Put up for sale after Bethell's departure, the property failed to find a buyer until 1984. It was then purchased by Robert Sangster, who proposed to install the leading jumping trainer, Michael Dickinson, at Whatcombe as his private trainer. In an extraordinary turn around, reputedly brought about by problems regarding the leases on the gallops, Sangster bought the Wiltshire training establishment of Manton, a property he had always desired, when the owner John Bloomfield dropped the price considerably. Sangster quickly contacted Paul Cole, who had been an interested party before Sangster's purchase. A deal was soon struck with Cole's principal patron, the Saudi Fahd Salman, who become a major shareholder in conjunction with his trainer, who incidentally had coveted Whatcombe for many years before.

Much renovation and building occurred. A new yard was built to house Cole's 100 horse string, far more than Budgett had ever trained. A new all weather gallop was constructed in a paddock close to the yard. An indoor school was erected to prevent the horses losing exercise time in bad weather. The property soon rivalled the most modern of establishments anywhere in the country. Cole moved his string from Lambourn in 1985. Whatcombe was in business again.

Fahd Salman did not have to wait long for a return on his investment. In 1990 Cole won him the Irish Oaks with Knight's Baroness, who had run third in the English equivalent, gaining some compensation for the

Irish Derby defeat of Insan the previous year. Cole scored his first domestic Classic win when Snurge, ridden by his former apprentice Richard Quinn, beat Hellenic in the Leger at Doncaster.

As Whatcombe basked in the glory of the Leger win, October saw Cole win the leading two-year-old race, the Dewhurst, with the 50–1 shot Generous. Whatcombe went into winter quarters with a live candidate for the 1991 Classic races. The Caerleon colt thrived in the winter and Cole decided to send him to the 2,000 Guineas without a run, happy that the outstanding Whatcombe training grounds were an ample substitute for a racecourse appearance. Generous ran fourth in the Guineas, finishing strongly, without experiencing much luck in running. Experienced judges believed him to have run a most promising Derby trial, although his owner Fahd Salman reputedly was less than happy with the ride Quinn had given Generous at Newmarket. Rumour was transformed to fact when a week later it was announced that Salman was to retain the young jockey Alan Munro, then attached to Bill O'Gorman's Newmarket stable, to ride all his horses. Salman's decision was to hit Richard Quinn hard, as he believed Generous to have been outpaced at Newmarket, patently needing a longer trip: an assumption that was to be proved correct.

Cole was happy to keep Generous off the track until Derby day. A searching gallop on Newbury racecourse two weeks before the Derby saw the flashy chestnut answer all the questions his trainer needed to ask. Whatcombe approached Epsom with confidence as a result of the racecourse gallop. Worries that his new jockey was too inexperienced for a Classic race proved unfounded, Munro and Generous spreadeagling the field to win in facile fashion. Victory in the Irish Derby followed. Generous proved in no uncertain terms in the King George at Ascot that he was a Derby winner of the highest class, when routing the best the older generation could muster.

Taken home to freshen up for his Arc de Triomphe quest he satisfied his connections in his work. At Longchamp he faded after looking dangerous in the straight. Like others before, the long summer campaign had taken its toll. Although a tilt at the Champion Stakes was at one time considered a possibility, Cole's experienced work rider Tommy Jennings, reported the colt to have trained off after partnering him in a gallop. Generous was retired to stud, the principal contributor towards his trainer's first ever Trainers' Championship. Although 1991 will be remembered

Paul Cole – the Master of Whatcombe

as Generous's year, Cole achieved a formidable result at the Royal Ascot meeting in June when winning all three two-year-old races open to colts, for Fahd Salman. Cole started 1992 with his biggest ever string. It is pertinent to note that Cole believes his rise to his present prominent position would not have been possible without Salman's patronage. He notes he would have fewer than eighty horses without Arab support. In a recent interview the tall, shy trainer commented somewhat wistfully: 'I'm glad I'm not starting now. I feel it is now a hundred times harder to get going' – a statement many of his younger less fortunate colleagues will understand only too well.

In 1949 Jack Colling took over Eric Stedall's lease on the Hodcott House establishment at West Ilsley, as a tenant of the Lockinge Estate, and moved his string to Berkshire from Newmarket, where he had trained with success since his retirement from riding at the end of the First World War. Among the patrons who moved from Newmarket was Lord Astor.

His famous gelding High Stakes, who had won seven successive races in 1946, moved to Ilsley with Colling. High Stakes, who continued to race until 1951 when he was nine years old, won thirty-four races in all. It was he who prompted his trainer to say that if he had a yard full of geldings, he would have run every race in the calendar. In 1952 Lord Astor died, leaving his substantial racing and bloodstock interests to his eldest son, Bill, and a younger son, John, known as Jakie. It was for the new Lord Astor that Colling was to train his only Classic winner in a long distinguished career, winning the 1953 Oaks with Ambiguity, ridden by the nineteen-year-old apprentice, Joe Mercer. Mercer's win on Ambiguity in the first year of his retainer with Colling's stable was to be the start of an association with Hodcott House, which was to be unbroken for the next twenty-three years. Further success for the Mercer/Colling partnership followed. In 1956 they won the Yorkshire Oaks for Jakie Astor with Indian Twilight. In 1959 the same owner's Rosalba won the Queen Elizabeth II Stakes at Ascot. In 1961 Jakie Astor's Escort won the Royal Lodge at Ascot, and went into winter quarters a strong fancy for the next years' Classic races. Escort proved to be a disappointment as a three-year-old in 1962, and at the end of that season Jack Colling announced his retirement. Hodcott House, which Colling had purchased a few years earlier from Christopher Loyd's Lockinge estate, was bought by Jakie Astor. The famous gallops continued to be leased from the Lockinge estate by Hodcott, as they are to this day.

Astor approached Dick Hern, who was training privately for Major Holliday, at Lagrange in Newmarket, to take over the sixty-two horses previously in Colling's care. Hern accepted and moved to Hodcott in the winter of the same year in which he had sent Holliday's Hethersett to win the St Leger at Doncaster. Astor proceeded to make his new acquisition the most modern training place of the time in Berkshire. He built one of the first indoor schools and constructed a private trotting road in the grounds of Hodcott for winter work. He built new hostel facilities with the proviso that they should be more comfortable then his trainer's accommodation! He purchased the Old Rectory in the village for Hern to live in, Jack Colling remaining in the house in the yard. Numerous cottages were purchased and renovated for stable staff. Hodcott, which had previously shared its facilities with a thriving Lockinge farmyard, became the showpiece establishment it is today.

Hern's first season at Hodcott was successful by any standards. He won sixty-two races in 1963. In 1964 he won the Doncaster Cup with Lord Astor's fine stayer Grey of Falloden, and the Zetland Gold Cup with Jakie Astor's Red Tears. 1965 saw Hern reward his patron Jakie Astor with his first Classic success, when Provoke, ridden by Joe Mercer, beat the odds-on Meadow Court in the St Leger, a race Hern was to plunder with monotonous regularity throughout his career. As Jakie Astor watched his homebred colt sluice home, his daughter Stella, less than keen on racing, visited a fortune teller at the fair in the centre of the course. She was informed that soon great fortune would fall on a close member of her family. As she emerged from the dark little tent, she saw Provoke's number placed on the board as the winner. The gypsy lady had made an accurate prediction.

A virulent virus attack affected Hern's yard in 1966, and for much of the season Hodcott barely sent out a runner. This was the first year that Hern received a consignment of yearlings from the Queen, who had sent six horses to Hodcott after a long association with her Newmarket trainer, Captain Cecil Boyd-Rochfort, had ended on his retirement. The next year saw a recovery and Jakie Astor's Remand, after winning the Royal Lodge, seemed a genuine Derby contender. However, the dreaded virus was to strike again next year. Although Remand finished fourth in the Derby to Sir Ivor, the disease was already incubating. Brought to its climax by the pressures of a race, the horse became sick and missed the rest of the season.

In 1970 Jakie Astor, on hearing that Sir Gordon Richards's lease was not going to be renewed at Whitsbury by the bookmaker William Hill, approached Sir Arnold Weinstock, who with his father-in-law Sir Michael Sobell, were Richards's principal patrons. Astor explained to Weinstock that he had decided to sell Hodcott as it was so expensive to run, and as his son Mickey was not interested in racing. He suggested to Weinstock that he should buy the stables lock, stock and barrel, solving the problem of where to have his string trained next year in one fell swoop. The deal was concluded with the minimum of fuss, and Weinstock became the new owner of Hodcott with Dick Hern remaining as trainer. Richards himself retired to manage the family's racing interests. The transference of ownership did not affect the stables in the least. The arrival in the winter of 1969 of a yearling colt by Queen's Hussar out of La Paiva saw to that.

The colt, named Brigadier Gerard, was to prove the most complete racehorse that Hern was to handle in his career. Bred by his owner, the former leading amateur rider and journalist John Hislop in partnership with his wife Jean, the breeding of Brigadier Gerard was a local affair. His sire Queen's Hussar stood at Highclere, only a mile or two from the Hislops' home at East Woodhay, near Newbury. Brigadier Gerard, who had consistently pleased Hern at home, was sent to Newbury for his debut in June 1970. Starting at 100–7 he slaughtered his field by five lengths. Further success at Salisbury and Newbury persuaded Hern that the colt was well up to group race standard. He was dispatched to Newmarket to win the Middle Park by a comfortable three lengths from the very fast two-year-old Swing Easy. It was his last run of the season. His owners, confident of their horse's ability, turned down an offer of £250,000 that winter.

The following spring, Hern was confident that he could produce Brigadier Gerard fit enough to win the Guineas first time out. The trainer has always believed that spring reaches Berkshire later than other areas. Consequently he felt that a racecourse outing before the Classic would do more harm than good. Hern, as in the case of Highclere and Nashwan, other first time out Guineas winners from Hodcott, produced the Brigadier at his peak at Newmarket. In one of the best Guineas ever run, Mercer produced the colt over a furlong out to win comfortably from the subsequent Derby winner Mill Reef, the favourite, with My Swallow third. Brigadier Gerard's next outing was in the St James's Palace at Royal Ascot. On soft ground he hated, he beat Sparkler by a head. At Goodwood he won the Sussex Stakes with ease from the French horse Faraway Son. Facile victories in the Goodwood Mile and the Queen Elizabeth II prompted his connections to try him in the mile-and-a-quarter Champion Stakes in October. Heavy conditions again forced him to have to fight, prevailing by the shortest of heads from the Paddy Prendergast-trained Rarity.

His four-year-old year was even more impressive. His only outing over a mile-and-a-half, the King George VI and Queen Elizabeth, saw him stay well enough, beating Parnell by a length and a half. His next outing at York was to be his only defeat. The Derby winner Roberto, ridden by the Panamanian jockey Braulio Baeza, deputizing for Piggott, who preferred to ride Rheingold, set a blistering pace. The Brigadier found the concession of 11 lb. beyond him, failing to overhaul Roberto by three lengths. Some critics thought the bubble had burst, claiming Hern had gone to the well once too often. However, Brigadier Gerard was to prove subsequently that he was as good as ever. His final two races, the Queen Elizabeth II and the Champion Stakes, he won with consummate ease. Retired to the Egerton Stud, Newmarket, the winner of seventeen of his eighteen races, he had proved himself in the highest class from two to four years old over all distances. There is little doubt he was the best race-horse ever trained in Berkshire. For sheer consistency he had no peer. Strangely, his stallion career was unsuccessful: he could not transmit his quality or talent to his progeny. Some pundits argue that he was a freak; like The Tetrarch, the type of horse one only sees once in a lifetime.

Two years later, Hern and Mercer were to win two Classics in a single year. Highclere beat the subsequent Oaks winner, Polygamy, in a thrilling finish to take the 1,000 Guineas, providing Hern with a first royal Classic victory. In September, Lady Beaverbrook's Bustino, destined a year later to star in the great drama of Grundy's King George victory, won the St Leger, a race Hern had informed the press months before was the Busted's horse's three-year-old target.

Joe Mercer ended his long association as retained jockey at Hodcott at the end of the 1976 season. At the Derby meeting in June it was announced by Weinstock that Willie Carson, then retained by Clive

Joe Mercer

Brittain's Newmarket stable, would succeed Mercer in the post he had held since 1953. Such was the shock the racing world suffered at the news that *The Times* saw fit to run the story in their front page columns. The Weinstock family, who owned the stables and the majority of the horses, called the tune. There was nothing Hern, the Queen or Jakie Astor could do, although they were all reputedly less than ecstatic at Weinstock's decision. Ironically Joe Mercer's departure from West Ilsley resulted in an approach from the powerful Newmarket stable of Henry Cecil. Mercer signed as Cecil's retained rider for the 1977 season. Two years later he was to win his only Riders' Championship, riding 164 winners. In 1981 Mercer moved back to Berkshire and rode for Peter Walwyn's Lambourn stable, only a few miles from where he had started as an apprentice in Major Sneyd's Sparsholt yard in 1947. The racing world applauded when in 1981 he won the St Leger on Cut Above for the team he had served for so long, Jakie Astor and Dick Hern. Mercer retired in 1985, winning the November Handicap on his last ever ride Bold Rex. He now manages the racing interests of Maktoum al Maktoum as well as running the farm at Hermitage where he has lived for many years.

If Mercer's departure from Hodcott was the end of an era, the arrival of the garrulous little Scottish rider Willie Carson was the beginning of another. In 1977 the Queen's Dunfermline provided Hern and his new stable jockey with dual Classic success, winning the Oaks and the St Leger. Her Oaks victory had been believed by some to be fortunate, as the favourite Durtal had been withdrawn after injuring herself in the preliminaries. Her Leger victory though was a performance of true class. She outstayed the subsequent Arc de Triomphe winner, Alleged, to win in a memorable struggle by a length. Although Dunfermline was kept in training at four, like many fillies of that age she failed to maintain her form – a second in the Hardwicke Stakes being her best effort.

In 1979 Hern and Carson won their first Derby. Carson rewarded the Weinstock family's faith in him by driving Troy to a seven-length victory in the 200th running of the race. Bred at Michael Sobell's Ballymacoll Stud in Ireland, Troy had proved a very useful two-year-old, winning the Royal Lodge at Ascot. A less than convincing win in the Sandown Classic trial left Carson undecided which of Hern's representatives he should ride at Epsom. Troy's impressive performance in the Predominate at Goodwood, when he beat Serge Lifar by seven lengths, made up the jockey's mind. He deserted the impressive Lingfield trial winner Milford and plumped for Troy. Troy went from strength to strength after his Epsom triumph, winning the Irish Derby, the King George and the Benson and Hedges. An odds-on favourite for the Arc he finished third to Three Troikas. Carson believed the soft ground had beaten Troy, reporting the big horse too heavy to handle it. Troy was sent to Highclere Stud for a tragically brief career. By May 1983 the great horse was dead as a result of a perforated gut.

1980 proved another golden year for Hodcott. Henbit won the Derby for Mrs Plesch, who had owned the 1961 66–1 winner Psidium. Henbit, an impressive winner of the Chester Vase before the Derby, started at the shorter price of 7–1. As he took the lead from Rankin Henbit appeared home and dry, until a furlong from the line he faltered and hung briefly to the right. Straightened up by Carson he ran on to hold Master Willie by three-quarters of a length. It transpired that Henbit had broken a bone in his leg when he had faltered. Bravely he had battled on to win. Henbit returned to training as a four-year-old patched up by the miracles of veterinary science but he was never the same again. Epsom week finished on a high note when Hern won the Oaks for Dick Hollingsworth with Bireme. Sadly the filly was injured in a training accident after Epsom and never ran again. Victory with the Guy Harwood cast-off Ela-Mana-Mou in the King George saw Hern end up champion trainer for the 1980 season for the third time.

In 1983 Hern and Carson had a further dual Classic winner when the filly Sun Princess won both the Oaks and the Leger for Sir Michael Sobell. In 1984 disaster was to strike West Ilsley. Dick Hern, hunting in his beloved Leicestershire, took a heavy fall on 7 December which broke his neck. By a strange quirk of fate a similar accident had befallen his Hodcott House predecessor Captain Richard Gooch before the war, confining the captain to a wheelchair for the remaining ten years of his life. The day after, partially paralysed, Hern was carefully transferred to Stoke Mandeville Hospital and placed in traction for the next six weeks. After an operation in February, he was discharged in April and returned home to West Ilsley. Although at first confined to a wheelchair, with daily two hour physiotherapy the trainer proved his resilience. In six months he was walking around his house with assistance. A specially designed red Mercedes van transported him to the gallops to supervise his string. In July Hern proved to any doubters that none of his legendary training ability had been lost when he saddled Lady Beaverbrook's

Petoski to win the King George VI and Queen Elizabeth at Ascot. The improvement Hern had conjured from the colt since his previous win in the Prince of Wales Stakes was evidence that the trainer was still a force to be reckoned with.

In 1988 Hern had to undergo major heart surgery in a London hospital. Neil Graham, who was to replace Alex Scott as Hern's assistant, returned from America early to take up his position. At the beginning of September it was announced that Graham would take over the licence for the rest of the season as Hern's doctors had ordered complete rest. Although Graham was the official trainer, Hern's finger was on the pulse: he was constantly on the telephone to his various staff. That autumn Hodcott won the St Leger with Lady Beaverbrook's Minster Son, bred by his rider Willie Carson. Cheers resounded around the winners' enclosure when Lady Beaverbrook reminded television viewers and pressmen not to forget Dick Hern. Prince of Dance deadheated with the Barry Hills-trained Scenic in the Dewhurst in October. Unfuwain ran a gallant fourth in the Arc at Longchamp. Al Hareb scored conclusively in the Futurity at Doncaster to show that Hodcott had strength in depth for the Classics next year. Hern on his return from hospital was a happy man.

In the winter months Hern believed his 2,000 Guineas horse to be the Futurity winner Al Hareb. However, a long striding colt by Blushing Groom out of Height of Fashion, Nashwan, who had won at Ascot in October, was soon to become the apple of his trainer's eye, when the string began cantering in the spring of 1989. In the New Year Nashwan had been lame as a result of splint trouble. The rest prescribed put him a month behind his stable companions. Al Hareb and Prince of Dance were in full work but not impressing as Classic horses should. Nashwan, however, recovered from his setback, was sparkling. Hern was still undecided whether to send Nashwan to the Guineas or to wait for Epsom. Although heavy betting on Nashwan for the Guineas was a feature of early April, it was not until a work-out a week after Newbury's Greenham meeting that Hern decided to send Nashwan to Newmarket.

The work over a mile with the good class handicapper Misbah was later described by Brian Proctor, Hern's long serving work rider as the best gallop he had ever taken part in at Ilsley. Sent a mile Misbah led Nashwan a strong pace for 6 furlongs. Carson then set Nashwan alight to go well clear over the last 2 furlongs. Hern later said he had never seen a horse work as well at Ilsley in his long career. The news of Nashwan's sensational gallop was soon public knowledge; Nashwan was backed to take vast sums out of the ring at Newmarket.

Although the home performances of the chestnut colt brought smiles to the trainer's face, since March he had been a worried man. An announcement during Cheltenham week from Buckingham Palace had stunned the racing world. The Queen, who had bought Hodcott some seven years before from the Weinstocks, announced that Hern's lease on the stables would not be renewed. She had appointed William Hastings-Bass, the godson of her racing manager, Lord Porchester, to take Hern's place at West Ilsley. Hastings-Bass had trained horses for the Queen from his Newmarket stables since 1977. The whys and wherefores of this strange decision will be discussed in a later chapter, but the fact remains that at the time Dick Hern was working under tremendous outside pressure. The trainer, his string and staff simply had no idea where they would be at the end of the season.

In the light of these events the whole of the racing world hoped in earnest that Nashwan would provide Hern with something to smile about at Newmarket. They were not to be disappointed. Nashwan, by then the 3–1 favourite, surged past Exbourne's pacemaker Greensmith over two furlongs out. Devouring the rising ground with his massive stride, Carson was not hard-pressed to hold off Exbourne by a length. The unsaddling enclosure was bedlam. Even the most hard nosed professionals struggled to greet the wheelchair-bound trainer to offer their congratulations. Hern announced his horse would gallop down the side of a house. Epsom was the next stop: the gradients would hold no fears for the athletic son of Blushing Groom.

The remainder of Nashwan's three-year-old career is the stuff of racing legend. His homework continued to confound his connections with its brilliance. Nobody wanted to know any other horse but Nashwan at Epsom. Starting at 5–4, he won by a facile five lengths from the outsider Terimon, with the likes of Cacoethes trailing in his wake. Hern announced he was the best horse he had ever trained, expressing doubts that Brigadier Gerard would have won the Derby at three. His next race, the Eclipse at Sandown, saw him prove Hern's analysis corrrect. In an incredible performance, fully eight lengths behind the pacemaker Opening Verse when turning for home, he strode clear up the Sandown hill to beat a top-class field of older horses by five lengths. In the King George at Ascot, Cacoethes got much closer than at Epsom, going down by only

Nashwan and Willie Carson returning in triumph after winning the 1989 2,000 Guineas.
The trainer Dick Hern is in the wheelchair

a neck to Nashwan. Carson, on dismounting, reported 'He just wasn't himself today.'

The King George was to be his last victory. Although his trainer Dick Hern favoured a crack at the St Leger before the Arc, his owner, Hamdan Al Maktoum, was anxious to train the horse specifically for an attempt at the Longchamp race. Given a rest after Ascot, Nashwan was aimed at Longchamp's Prix Neil, a recognized Arc trial run three weeks before the big French race. The famous acceleration failed to manifest; Nashwan was only third to the Jonathan Pease-trained Golden Pheasant, an animal way below Nashwan in class. Taken home to Ilsley, it was soon known that the colt would miss the Arc and be prepared for the Champion Stakes. Four days before the race it was announced that Nashwan had a temperature and would not fulfil his Newmarket engagement. He was retired to his owner's Shadwell Stud in Norfolk. The great horse had run his last race.

In the preceding May, Buckingham Palace had announced that Hern could continue at Hodcott for one more year to give him time to find

Mr Frisk, the 1990 Grand
National winner, at Kim Bailey's
Old Manor Stables, Upper Lambourn

Three of Paul Cole's horses galloping on Whatcombe's famous Woolley Down

Paul Cole's horses leaving Whatcombe for the gallops

Whatcombe – Paul Cole's string returning from exercise

Nicky and Diana Henderson on the Mandown gallops, Lambourn

Remittance Man and Richard Dunwoody in full flight

new premises. He would share the yard and facilities with Hastings-Bass. Later in 1989 Hamdan Al Maktoum, Nashwan's grateful owner, caused the racing world to breathe a sigh of relief. The sheikh announced that he would build Hern new stables to continue his career. In 1990 Hern narrowly failed to add a transatlantic first to his distinguished record. The great sprinter Dayjur forfeited a certain win in the Breeders' Cup Sprint when jumping a shadow close to the line. After much searching, the Kingwood stables of the retired trainer Mark Smyly were purchased. Set on the hill on the Hungerford Road out of Lambourn, millions of pounds were spent rebuilding the yard and renovating the gallops. Two years ago the trainer moved to his new base from where Mark Smyly had sent out the 1977 Lincoln winner Blustery. He is still awaiting the arrival of a top-class horse. His successor at Hodcott, William Hastings-Bass, now Lord Huntingdon, continued the stable's tradition by saddling two successive winners of the Ascot Gold Cup, Indian Queen in 1991 and Drum Taps in 1992.

The achievements of Dick Hern during his twenty-eight year tenure at West Ilsley make staggering reading. Fifteen British Classic wins fell to the stable during Hern's time as well as five King Georges. Triumphs were also attained from the sprinting field through to the great staying races. Famous stayers like Sea Anchor, Little Wolf and Longboat, milers like Sallust and Sun Prince, sprinters like Lady Beaverbrook's grand old gelding Boldboy and more recently Dayjur spring readily to mind. Hern's stable is run, in the way of the old school, in strict regimental fashion, staff and horses knowing exactly what is required. Hern inspires great loyalty. Only two jockeys, Mercer and Carson, were retained by Hodcott in Hern's time. This loyalty is extended to his staff, who stand by him through thick and thin. Although sometimes less than open with the press, Hern believes he answers only to his owners. Set in the mould of trainers of the past, his like is a disappearing breed. Jakie Astor can no doubt reflect with pleasure his decision to tempt Hern from Newmarket way back in 1962.

The great man is of a somewhat superstitious nature. A revolving statue of a naked lady stands in a lake alongside the M3 motorway. Hern travels to the racecourses on that route with trepidation. For he knows that if the lady has turned bashfully away, hiding her notable natural assets, he will miss out on a winner. If, however, he is greeted by her full frontal view, the trainer continues on his way knowing fortune will favour him.

Some years ago Hern knew a small local trainer was exercising his few horses illegally on the famous Hodcott turf. Hard though he tried Hern could not catch him in the act. One day he rang the intruder to warn him off the gallops. Bold as brass the trainer retorted that neither he nor his horses had set foot on them at any time. One day at the crack of dawn the trainer sent a horse to exercise at Hern's. The unfortunate animal suffered a stroke and fell down dead in the middle of the gallop. His lad, terrified of encountering Hern, set off in a panic for home, leaving his mount still saddled and bridled in its final resting place. Sure enough Hern found the horse when his string arrived to exercise minutes later. Mindful of his last conversation with the trainer he rang him when he returned to breakfast. The rather one-sided conversation went as follows:

Hern: 'The most extraordinary thing happened this morning. While exercising my string, I found one of your horses dead in the middle of the gallops with its tack on. It must have disposed of its jockey on your gallops, run the mile towards mine, fallen to its knees and dropped dead.'

The trainer, speechless for a moment, said he would remove it straight away. Hern never recalled seeing his string on Hodcott ground again!

Although the neighbouring village of East Ilsley had no horse of its nineteenth-century resident Lord Lyon's capabilities, old Commissar as we have heard, landed a mighty gamble in the Lincoln of 1948. A great trial before the race saw Commissar beaten a neck by George Beeby's Lincoln hope Fleckton, trained at nearby Compton. Arthur Budgett reputedly was so pleased with the trial that the stable money went down. Commissar turned the tables on the Beeby horse at Lincoln. Ridden by Bill Rickaby he scored by two lengths with Fleckton only third. The stable took some £40,000 out of the ring that day and apparently Budgett financed his purchase of Whatcome thanks to Commissar.

Before Budgett bought the Nelson House establishment, it was the property of a splendid character named Tommy Cross. Just after the war Cross trained a good handicapper, The Little Topper. Cross laid him out for one of the big Ascot handicaps, putting an apprentice, John Terry, aboard to take some weight off the old horse's back. Terry, who later trained in Scandinavia, was delighted to beat Sir Gordon Richards in a close finish to record his first ever winner. His delight was somewhat tempered when he discovered that the great jockey had invested on The Little Topper hearing what a certainty he was. Tommy Cross fell on hard times, later working on the fencing when Hodcott was developed by Jakie Astor. Nelson House has now been developed for housing. Roddy Armytage trained many decent jumpers there in the sixties and seventies.

Across the road the Kennet House stables housed the most famous ringer of all. Francascal, who won a Bath seller in the early fifties, was actually a ringer for a far superior French horse. Both horses were bought in France at the same time and identities were swopped. The coup was only discovered as a man was seen cutting the telephone wires connecting Bath racecourse to the outside world, to prevent the huge sums invested getting back to the track. The real Francascal is reputed to be buried somewhere in the Kennet House yard. The authorities did not look kindly on the coup, the trainer being warned off for many years. Of course the bookmakers refused to pay out when the trick was discovered.

In 1965 Gavin Hunter went to Kennet House to train privately for Captain Langton, who had purchased the establishment from Syd Warren. Hunter trained some decent horses there in a twenty-year career becoming a public trainer in 1970. He won the 1977 Doncaster Cup with Shangamuzzo and landed a notable gamble when Greenwood Star won the Jubilee of 1981. In 1985 Hunter retired, a victim of bad debts and rising costs. He sold Kennet House to his assistant Martin Fetherston-Godley, who is the only flat trainer in East Ilsley at the present time.

Kim Bailey's yard at Hill House is empty and still awaiting a buyer two years after the trainer's move to Lambourn. Bailey's predecessor Charlie Dingwall once had a prospective owner coming down. Dingwall had two horses to sell so to facilitate identification he made their riders wear different coloured caps. Instructing his work riders to make sure the horses he wished to sell finished in front in the gallop, he set off with the prospective owner to the finishing place on the downs. Alighting from his Land Rover he told the man to watch carefully the riders with the coloured caps, as they were sure to breast the rise in front. As the horses shot by the owner was unable to pick out the relevant horses. Later it transpired that both his prospective purchases had whipped round at the start, depositing their jockeys on the ground!

Two other racing yards in East Ilsley have gone for building or residential occupation. Churchill House was once the quarters of Basil Briscoe, who trained the great steeplechaser Golden Miller at his previous base in Cambridgeshire. Jimmy James trained principally for Lord Cadogan in the village. James, who once trained privately for Major Holliday, reputedly saved Lord Cadogan's life in the war. His Lordship generously rewarded James by sending him horses for many years. Simon Sherwood has recently built a splendid new establishment on the Compton side of East Ilsley increasing the horse population of the famous village.

If there was a shortage of class flat horses in East Ilsley in the post-war period, the neighbouring village of Compton, without turning out a Classic winner, housed many decent animals. In 1947 Ken Cundell purchased Roden House stables and soon assembled a decent mixed string. In 1951 Cundell had won the Blue Riband at Epsom with Zucchero: the temperamental colt was later moved to Bill Payne's Lambourn stable. One of his first good horses was the high-class sprinter March Past, who won the Solario in 1952, the Greenham in 1953 and the Wokingham of 1954. March Past was owned by Mrs Trimmer Thompson, whose stud was where Khaled Abdullah's Juddmonte stud is today.

Ascot was to prove a lucky track for Cundell. Firstling won the Britannia at the Royal meeting in 1951 and Grass Court won the Cork and Orrery in 1954. In 1962 Cundell won the Cork and Orrery again with Nereus and the 1968 Victoria Cup with Rome. Haydock Park's Vernons Sprint was also to prove a lucky race for Cundell's stable. In 1973 he scored with Lady Clifden's Golden Orange and in 1974 in his final year training won again with Wilfrid Sherman's Princely Son. In the sixties Cundell had a good old stayer, Chiseldon. As he advanced in years the old horse sometimes declined to jump off. One day he was in a two horse race. Shrewd punters backed the other horse knowing they were on a winner either way. If Chiseldon jumped off, they would take a price about him in running. The old fellow declined to race, the other animal, Knotty Pine, later to win an Ebor Handicap, finishing alone.

Ken Cundell retired in 1974 and handed over his stables to his son Peter, who trained the fine sprinter King of Spain and the Chester Cup winner Contester in 1984. In his heyday Ken Cundell trained a large mixed string occupying two yards in Compton. These days his son Peter trains very few horses. He is the President of the National Trainers Federation and the racing advisor to the television series *Trainer*, which is filmed in the Hamilton House yard that his father Ken bought from George Beeby in the early seventies.

In 1958 Ken Cundell leased his Yew Tree Stables yard to the former amateur rider Atty Corbett, son of the chief scout Lord Rowallan.

Corbett won some good races during the ten years he trained in Compton. In 1963 he won the Gimcrack and the Champagne Stakes with the flying two-year-old Talahasse, and in 1966 the Free Handicap with Kibenka. But the best horse he had in his time there was undoubtedly Lord Carnarvon's Queen's Hussar, later to find fame as the sire of Brigadier Gerard. After a tough two-year-old campaign in 1962, winning four times from nine races, he improved at three, scoring in the Lockinge and Sussex stakes. As a four-year-old he won the Cavendish at Sandown before being retired to the Highclere Stud. Queen's Hussar was a son of Ken Cundell's first good horse March Past. Corbett was tragically killed in a road accident in 1976 in Newmarket, while walking with his string.

George Beeby, who will figure in the steeplechasing chapter of this book in detail, changed the emphasis of his training towards the flat in the later years of his career. The best horse he trained at Hamilton House, Compton, was Grey Sovereign, a very useful sprinter in the early fifties. Grey Sovereign, by Nasrullah, was a temperamental sort. Much of his training was done on the endless tracks around the Ridgeway. These days the huge modern tractors have ruined these once perfect tracks. Beeby also won the Stewards Cup in 1957 with Arcandy and the 1941 Cambridgeshire with Rue de Paix. One of his last good winners was the 1965 Wokingham victor Nunshony, ridden by David East. Beeby retired in 1971 and died in 1977. His last runner at Newmarket, Grey Gaston, was a winner.

Presently David Arbuthnot is the only trainer in Compton besides Peter Cundell. He leases the Yew Tree Stables yard from the Cundells, having previously been at Hamilton stables further up the village. Arbuthnot, who was assistant to Fulke Johnson-Houghton at Blewbury, has won some good races from Compton in recent times. His Rinja won the Bessborough at Royal Ascot and the good sprinter Love Legend took Doncaster's Portland Handicap.

Other famous stables to the east are gone. Michael Pope trained some good horses at Streatley, where he moved in the middle sixties from Blewbury. Sky Rocket won the Wokingham for Pope in 1969 ridden by Pat Eddery. It was Pope who provided Eddery with his first ever winner Alvara earlier that year. Pope specialized in keeping old handicappers sweet. Birdbrook, who won sixteen races, was a fine example, as was old Pheidippides who went on winning for years. Pope used to send his two-year-olds to be trained at Frank Cundell's Aston Tirrold yard where there

Two Berkshire trainers – Tim Thomson-Jones of Lambourn (left) and David Arbuthnot of Compton

were better facilities for them. Not many trainers would dare to do that in the cut-throat atmosphere of the modern day. Pope retired in 1973 to manage the racing interests of his principal owner Lord McAlpine, and was President of the Trainers Federation for many years.

Norah Wilmot's stable at Binfield Grove is no longer. Miss Wilmot trained until a year before her death aged ninety-one in 1980. Her best post-war horse was No Fiddling who won the 1961 Blue Riband and five other races that year. In September 1964 Miss Wilmot won a race for the Queen at Folkestone with Don't Tell. The Ascot Cottage Stables at Winkfield are also gone. From there Doug Marks sent out Golden Fire to win the Cesarewitch, the Goodwood Stakes and the Chester Cup of 1962. Con Horgan now trains not far from Binfield at Billingbear. He won the 1985 Ebor with Western Dancer. His is now the only public stable in the Ascot area.

5
STEEPLECHASING – THE SECOND WORLD WAR TO THE PRESENT

Although Whatcombe and West Ilsley were the exclusive preserves of the the flat-race horse, the consistency with which Berkshire stables plundered the major prizes of National Hunt racing, the winter game, in the post-war period made the area the principal training place for the steeplechaser in the country. Reg Hobbs, the Rhonehurst trainer, brought the National Hunt Trainers' Championship to Lambourn in the 1941-2 season, capitalizing on the increased patronage that the 1938 Aintree triumph of Battleship had brought him. Medoc II who won the Cheltenham Gold Cup in the 1942 season was the principal contributor. Although jump racing, like its counterpart on the flat, was conducted on a much reduced scale in the war years, it was at this time that Fulke Walwyn was laying the foundations of a training career in Lambourn, which was to place his stable in the forefront of the winter game for the next fifty years.

Educated at Malvern, Walwyn's childhood on the Welsh borders was dominated by the horse. His formal riding education completed in the traditional manner in the hunting field, the early thirties saw the young Walwyn begin his career as an amateur rider under National Hunt rules. Success was quick to follow. Walwyn was leading amateur in the 1932-3 and 1933-4 seasons. Increasing success saw Walwyn riding for the major stables. In 1936, firmly established as one of the leading riders, Walwyn obtained the ride on Reynoldstown, the previous year's Grand National winner. Ridden in 1935 to victory by Frank Furlong, an unequal struggle against the scales prompted Furlong to offer his great friend the mount on the family horse. The partnership was an immediate success, Walwyn winning three races on Reynoldstown that season including the Grand National at Aintree. The same year saw Walwyn partner the great Golden Miller to victory in a Wincanton race, sowing the seeds of a partnership with that horse's owner Dorothy Paget, which was to benefit Walwyn's subsequent training career considerably.

Fulke Walwyn

Three years after Walwyn's greatest triumph his promising riding career was brought cruelly to a premature halt. An horrendous fall from Grosvenor Bridge in a minor race at little Ludlow on 19 April 1939 saw the rider forced to look for alternative employment. The beginning of the 1939-40 jump season saw the new trainer resident at Lambourn's famous old stable, Delamere House. After training eighteen winners in that first season, war this time played its hand. After this promising early start, at the end of that season Walwyn rejoined his old regiment. 1944 saw Walwyn return to Lambourn and in that year he purchased Ted Gwilt's Saxon House stables in Upper Lambourn. From Saxon House he was with regularity to train the winners of jumping's top prizes for more than forty years.

Walwyn rose rapidly to the head of his profession. For three successive years, from 1946 to 1949, Saxon House was the leading National Hunt stable in the country, with Walwyn taking the Trainers' Championship in these years. In the 1947–8 season he won seventy-five races, taking the Scottish Grand National and Kempton's King George with the chaser Rowland Roy in 1947. In 1948 he experienced victory at the Cheltenham Festival, winning the Cathcart with Jack Tatters. In 1949 the same horse won the amateur riders' race, the Kim Muir. On the hurdling front he won the Imperial cup for two years in a row in 1949 and 1950, with Secret Service.

Walwyn's principal patron in these early years was the notoriously difficult owner Dorothy Paget, the huge spinster daughter of Lord Queensborough. The inheritor of an enormous fortune from her maternal grandfather, the American millionaire William Whitney, Dorothy Paget was one of the biggest spenders on the turf from 1930 until her death in 1960. Although she won the 1943 Derby with Straight Deal, her successes in the jumping field were greater. Her most famous jumper was Golden Miller, who won five Gold Cups and a Grand National in the thirties. On one occasion when the great horse contested the National, Lord Queensborough is reputed to have turned to the horse's trainer, Basil Briscoe, on seeing a hare jump up and run down the course uttering the immortal words: 'Damn: there goes my daughter's last chance of a husband.'

Although Dorothy Paget was legendary for dismissing her trainers, her partnership with Walwyn lasted to the end of her life. Becoming even more eccentric she rarely went racing in her later years, preferring to stay at her house in Chalfont St Giles, sleeping most of the day. At night she would rise and consume enormous meals in the company of a posse of secretaries, employed to cater for her every whim. If her life style precluded her going racing she continued to follow the fortunes of her horses by endless late night telephone calls to her trainers, and examination of the photographs they sent her. She also continued to bet on her horses in staggering proportions even if their chance was negligible. On one occasion Walwyn saddled five winners in a row at Folkestone for her. When Bryan Marshall was beaten in the final race, Miss Paget, forgetting her earlier successes of the afternoon, could only comment: 'I'm very disappointed Lucky Monarch didn't win the last race.'

In 1952 Walwyn saddled the French horse Mont Tremblant to win the Cheltenham Gold Cup for Dorothy Paget. Ridden by Dave Dick, Mont Tremblant was Walwyn's most important jumping triumph for the eccentric lady and the trainer's first victory in steeplechasing's greatest race. Walwyn's victories for Dorothy Paget were not confined to National Hunt racing. In 1950 he won the Doncaster Cup with the winning hurdler Aldborough, and had charge of the fast two-year-old Wilma who was always ridden by Sir Gordon Richards. Although Dorothy Paget died in

Mandarin (Fred Winter) at the water during his famous victory in the Grand Steeplechase de Paris at Autueil. The broken bit is clearly visible

1960, the loss of her horses did not affect the Saxon House establishment. The sixties were to be the most important decade of Walwyn's career.

The great French-bred chaser Mandarin won the Gold Cup in 1962 for Saxon House. Sent unbroken to Walwyn in 1954, the popular horse strode up the Cheltenham Hill in the hands of Fred Winter to score by a length from Fortria. Sent to contest the Grand Steeplechase de Paris at Autueil in the land of his birth, worth at £20,000 some £14,000 more than the Cheltenham race, Mandarin's victory was the most dramatic in steeplechasing's history. Leading at the third fence, Fred Winter to his horror found the horse's new bit had broken in half. Devoid of steering Winter rode his greatest race, somehow negotiating the huge obstacles to prevail in the end by only a short head. Mandarin's victory in France was the culmination of a splendid year for Saxon House, the stable having also won the hurdling crown when Anzio took the Champion Hurdle.

To follow Mandarin, Saxon House had a new star waiting in the wings. Transferred from Syd Dale's Epsom yard by his owner Bill Gollings in the summer of 1962, the promising horse that Dale had purchased from Ireland quickly impressed his new trainer. A victory in a Sandown handicap under 10 st. 7 lb. was Mill House's first victory for Walwyn. A defeat at Kempton after a mistake at the last, which nearly unseated Willie Robinson, prompted some observers to suggest that Cheltenham's stiff fences would find out the novice on Gold Cup day.

Mill House was never in danger. Jumping into the lead at the water on the second circuit, he won by twelve lengths from the eternal bridesmaid, Fortria. The press were ecstatic in their praise, claiming a true champion had arrived. They said he would win the Gold Cup for years. In his final outing of 1963, he won the Mandarin at Newbury, prompting his jockey Robinson to describe him as a 'Rolls'. Mill House went to his summer break described as the best steeplechaser seen for years.

It was only the fact that Mill House was born in the same era as Arkle that prevented him from winning jumping's crown again. Although he won many top-class races until his retirement in 1968, including a Whitbread and a King George, he was destined to play second fiddle to the great Irish horse Arkle in the Gold Cup, finishing second to him on two occasions. Mill House's first defeat in the Gold Cup by Arkle left Walwyn a most disappointed man. Feeling Mill House to be by far the best horse he had trained, he could not believe how Arkle could dispose of him so easily.

During Mill House's time at Saxon House, the stable won the 1965 Champion Hurdle with the outsider Kirriemuir. A year before Walwyn won his only Grand National as a trainer, when Team Spirit triumphed at Aintree. Purple Silk looked to be the winner jumping the last. It was only after the Elbow that the tiny Team Spirit quickened under Willie Robinson. The verdict at the line was only half a length, reminiscent of an earlier Lambourn victory when another fifteen-hand horse, Battleship, had won in 1938.

Little Team Spirit's rider Willie Robinson was light for a jump jockey. Indeed he finished second in the Derby of 1958 on Paddy's Point. When he retired from riding he trained for a period on the Curragh, winning the Irish 2,000 Guineas with King's Company. The many falls he had in his distinguished jumping career left him somewhat absent minded. One year he brought a decent sprinter Bold Tack to lodge in Peter Walwyn's Seven Barrows yard, to take advantage of the greater opportunities for such a horse on this side of the Irish Sea. The day after Robinson's return to Ireland, Walwyn's head lad Ray Laing went to feed Bold Tack early in the morning. As he walked towards the manger, the horse savaged him, biting him several times in the leg. Terrified, Laing somehow escaped from the box. On hearing of the incident, the irate master of Seven Barrows telephoned Robinson to see if he could shed any light on Bold Tack's strange behaviour. After Walwyn had finished describing Laing's narrow escape, Robinson's response was: 'By Jesus, I knew there was something I'd forgotten to tell you when I left.'

In 1973, the year Fulke Walwyn first received the Queen Mother's horses after Peter Cazalet had died, Saxon House won a third Gold Cup with the huge headstrong former point to pointer The Dikler. Almost unrideable in his early days, constantly running out in his races, Walwyn found the key to The Dikler. He improved the horse's jumping, harness-ing and directing the son of Vulgan's undoubted talent in what was one of his greatest training performances. Ridden by Ron Barry, the immensely strong Irish rider, who alone could manage him, The Dikler

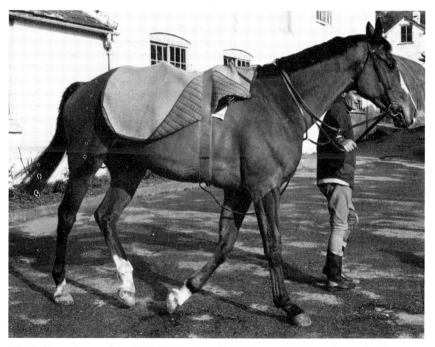

The Dikler, winner of the 1973 Cheltenham Gold Cup, with his regular work rider, Darkie Deacon

ran on strongly up the hill to overhaul the tiring Pendil to win by a short head. The King George winner in 1971 and third to Glencaraig Lady the year before, it had seemed to many that The Dikler had missed his chance. However Walwyn was a year later to win the Whitbread with the old horse on the disqualification of the John Oaksey-ridden Proud Tarquin. Oaksey was deemed to have interfered with Barry's mount on the steep Sandown run-in.

Although The Dikler was Saxon House's last triumph in the Cheltenham feature, Fort Devon, Diamond Edge and Ten Plus gave sterling performances in the race in the ensuing years. Ten Plus's fall when clear at the second last in Walwyn's penultimate training year of 1989, proved the great trainer still well capable of producing his charges at the top of their form for the big day – a feature of his runners throughout his long career. If the big Cheltenham races eluded Saxon House in the late seventies and eighties, formidable victories were achieved elsewhere. Diamond Edge won the Whitbread of 1979 and the Hennessy and Whitbread of 1981. In 1984 the Queen Mother's Special Cargo scored in an exciting finish for the Whitbread. Always this bad-legged horse provided testament to Walwyn's skill. Produced fit and fancied three years in a row, he won the Grand Military from 1984 to 1986. Among other notable achievements of the eighties was a six timer from six runners on 30 October 1981.

At the end of the 1990 season Fulke Walwyn finally handed over the Saxon House stables to his wife Cath, herself a daughter of the racehorse owner and breeder Sir Humphrey de Trafford. In 1991 Fulke Walwyn died. His wife Cath, with the Queen Mother still a patron, continues training at Saxon House. Fulke Walwyn's achievements during the long period he held a licence did much to attract attention to the village of Lambourn. It was his consistency in producing top-class steeplechasers over fifty years that really put the village on the jumping map. It has much to thank him for.

Nick Gaselee, the Lambourn trainer of the 1992 Grand National winner Party Politics, was Walwyn's assistant and amateur rider for many years. Gaselee believes the key to Walwyn's enduring success was an unique ability to pick out with rapidity the best way to train a particular horse. He cites the case of The Dikler as a good example. When the huge horse arrived, Walwyn was told he was such a tearaway that the only hope was to run him in two mile races, riding him from the front.

Within days Walwyn discounting this theory, set about settling down the explosive horse. With the help of his work rider Darkie Deacon, he taught the horse to relax behind his lead horses, conserving all his energy. Gaselee firmly believes that The Dikler would never have been heard of if he had not ended up in Walwyn's care.

Walwyn was not a great believer in the modern trend of loose-schooling. He preferred his young horses to learn to jump with a rider on their backs over baby hurdles in the paddocks behind his house. Not one for extensive schooling if an animal jumped well, like the Dickinsons, he only schooled his good chasers to get their eye in at the beginning of the year. Like the present-day champion trainer Martin Pipe, if Walwyn sent a horse to the racecourse, it was guaranteed to be fit.

In 1964 Mandarin's former jockey Fred Winter bought Charlie Pratt's old stable at Uplands from Doug Marks. Set up a tiny lane that wends towards the Mandown training grounds, the property's next door neighbour is the Walwyn yard at Saxon House. The former champion rider was a somewhat reluctant recruit to the training game. Originally Winter wanted to become a starter, but the Jockey Club in their wisdom made it clear they would not entertain his application. Winter's second choice career took off like lightning.

In his first season's training he won the Grand National with the American chaser Jay Trump. Twice the winner of America's most prestigious steeplechase, the Maryland Hunt Cup, Jay Trump and his rider Tommy Smith arrived at Uplands. Fred Winter's task was to prepare both horse and rider for the assault on Aintree. Jay Trump and his rider could hardly have acclimatized better. Three racecourse outings before Aintree resulted in victories. At Aintree the incredible dream was realized, Smith and Jay Trump beating the Scottish-trained Freddie by three-quarters of a length. Smith, showing commendable coolness for an amateur, gave Jay Trump a smack with his whip on the run-in. Feeling the horse hang, resenting the blow, he quickly put his whip down and rode hands and heels towards the line.

The very next year fortune was to favour the Uplands stable for a second time. Anglo, a horse decidedly inferior to Jay Trump, was Winter's representative in the National of 1966. Starting at 50–1, the horse, who had only arrived in Winter's yard as the trainer's old boss Ryan Price's licence had been withdrawn, showed vastly improved form, to win by twenty lengths in the hands of Tim Norman, with the gallant Freddie second again. Anglo, strangely, had won as a two-year-old. Then named Flag of Convenience, he carried the colours of Sir Randle Fielden. Bought later by Ryan Price for only £1,000, he became the property of the film producer Nat Cohen and his partner, Stuart Levy. Cohen had owned Kilmore, the last National winner that Fred Winter had ridden as a jockey.

If Anglo was not, by any stretch of the imagination, a horse of top class, Winter's performance in winning two Nationals in the first two years of his training career soon saw his yard full of animals of high potential. 1970 saw Winter win the Trainers' Championship, a title the Uplands stable was to claim for the next five years. In 1971 Bula, ridden by Paul Kellaway, won the Champion Hurdle, a race that was to feature on the agenda of the Uplands stable for the next few years. Bula was a champion hurdler of the highest class. Invariably settled a long way back by Kellaway, he consistently produced formidable powers of acceleration to dominate the hurdling field. In 1972 Bula regained his crown. Sent in his advancing years over fences, he adapted to become a steeplechaser of high standard, finishing second in the Gold Cup of 1975. Unlike many other top hurdlers he adapted to jumping the larger fences well. He failed to win a Gold Cup because he was not a true stayer of the Gold Cup distance. However, as a hurdler he had no chinks in his armoury.

Winter soon found a successor in the shape of Lord Howard de Walden's Lanzarote. Trained on the flat at Middleham by Ernie Weymes, he quickly adapted to the winter game. In 1974 he gave Winter a third Champion Hurdle in four years. Ridden by Richard Pitman, his victory suggested he could easily emulate his stable companion Bula and score in successive years. However, the Fred Rimell-trained Comedy of Errors, beaten by Lanzarote in 1974, was to prevent the Winter horse adding to his victory, dominating the race for the rest of Lanzarote's hurdling career. Sent over fences he never jumped as well as Bula, tending to flatten his obstacles. This trait was to prove his undoing. In Davy Lad's Gold Cup, Lanzarote slipped on landing at the seventh, sustaining injuries which were to prove fatal.

If Uplands farmed the Champion Hurdle in the early seventies, the Gold Cup was proving to be Winter's unlucky race. Failures with Bula and Lanzarote were preceded by the great chaser Pendil's inability to win the race. Beaten by a short head by The Dikler in 1973, he started a short priced favourite a year later, only to fall in the country, brought down by the indifferent jumper, High Ken. A year on, Winter and Pitman still could not lay the hoodoo to rest, Soothsayer finishing six lengths second to the Irish-trained Ten Up. 1978 saw Winter's luck change in the race. The last day of Cheltenham was abandoned due to snow, and the Gold Cup was reopened to be run in April. Mrs Olive Jackson's young Midnight Court barely out of his novice days beat the great Irish horse Brown Lad by seven lengths. The ground was firm that April day at Cheltenham and they went too fast for old Brown Lad. Sent clear by John Francome down the inside on the bend, Midnight Court was ten lengths clear at the last. Although Brown Lad finished strongly the Winter horse was home and hosed.

In the eighties the Uplands stable had some promising chasers. Venture To Cognac, Brown Chamberlain and the Sheik Ali Abu Khamsin-owned Fifty Dollars More won plenty of good races but the Gold Cup was to elude their grasp. On the hurdling front Celtic Shot showed high promise, but fate was to intervene to prevent Fred Winter training a fourth Champion Hurdle winner.

Fred Winter's training career was brought to an early close. After sustaining a stroke, Winter lost his power of speech. When recovery was deemed by his doctors to be unlikely he sold the Uplands establishment to his assistant Charlie Brooks, who had, with the help of Winter's daughter Joanna, kept Uplands running during Winter's illness. The young trainer was to saddle Celtic Shot to win the Champion Hurdle in his first season, as good a start as Winter had had twenty years earlier. The former champion jockey and trainer now lives quietly in the neighbouring village of Eastbury, reputedly following with interest the sport he graced for so long.

Winter believed John Francome to be the best rider to present a steeplechaser at a fence he had ever seen. When Francome arrived at Uplands he was a proven champion in the showjumping field. Taught the art of race riding by Winter, he was promoted as first jockey on Richard Pitman's retirement. Although Francome's finish was deemed weak by some in the early days, he developed this side of his riding to become one of the great champions. His Champion Hurdle win on Sea Pigeon was a fine example of the power he generated in a finish in his later years. Associated with the Winter stable for all his riding career, on his retirement he set up as a trainer at Sheepdrove south of Lambourn. On his announcement that he was to start the next season, a gentleman called on

Two great champion jump jockeys – John Francome (left) and Fred Winter

Francome with a view to sending him a horse. After a cup of tea and a discussion the man rose to take his leave. Telling Francome that he had enjoyed meeting him and would send him a horse, he was amazed to hear the prospective trainer say he did not want to train it. Francome explained that their short meeting had persuaded him that the unfortunate man was not his type at all. The great jockey trained for a brief period before turning to the fields of television and journalism. His Sheepdrove training yard is now leased by the Lambourn trainer Barry Hills.

Winter was apparently less than talkative at first lot in the morning, preferring action to words at that early hour. The jockeys he employed during his training career with the exception of Peter Scudamore, who replaced Francome, were not notable for their shyness. Richard Pitman and Francome make their livings on live television, a medium requiring endless verbosity. Paul Kellaway and E.P. Harty, earlier riders for the stable, are legendary in their ability to talk the hind leg off a donkey. It is intriguing to think what the trainer thought of the endless chatter on those early mornings.

One of the most popular horses Winter trained was the Australian chaser Crisp. Ironically, Crisp is best remembered for his defeat in the 1973 National rather than any race he won. His performance under the welterweight of 12 st. to run the great Aintree specialist Red Rum to three-quarters of a length was one of the National's finest. Fifteen lengths clear at the last, Crisp agonizingly faltered on the run-in to let Red Rum by close to the line. His jockey Richard Pitman, admitting to being as tired as his mount, could offer little assistance: Crisp had no more left to give. The exhilarating manner in which Crisp jumped the huge Aintree fences remains indelible on the minds of those who saw it. They will never witness such an exhibition again.

Although the Walwyn and Winter stables were responsible for the vast majority of class jumpers in Lambourn until the eighties, some good horses were housed in the village in the smaller yards. In 1963 the South Bank establishment of Keith Piggott won the National with Ayala. Owned by the hairdressing salon proprietor 'Teasy Weasy' Raymond, Ayala in 1963 was the first of the four successive winners Lambourn would have in the race. Ridden by Pat Buckley, Ayala with a stirring run deprived the Gay Kindersley-owned Carrickbeg, the mount of John Lawrence, later to become Lord Oaksey, of the spoils in the closing stages of the race. Unfancied at 66–1, Ayala had been bought by Keith Piggott for only £200 in 1960. Poor legs contributed to the cheap price. It was with difficulty that Piggott prepared Ayala for Aintree, running him in only three races before the day. It was to be Ayala's greatest moment. In his four subsequent outings he finished down the field.

As well as Francome and Winter, Lambourn since the war has seen several former champion jump jockeys try their luck at the training game. Bryan Marshall trained at Berkeley House and Jack Dowdeswell at Neardown. On the Wantage Road Stan Mellor bought the stables of George Spann in the early seventies. He won the Triumph Hurdle with Pollardstown and sent the good chaser Royal Mail to finish third in Aldaniti's National in 1981. Both horses were ridden by Mellor's stable jockey, Philip Blacker, later to find fame as an equine sculptor. Mellor sold his Linkslade stables in the late eighties and moved to the former stud, King Edward Place, where the ruined millionaire proprietor Jimmy White took his own life in 1927.

At Rhonehurst Richard Head, son of the distinguished cabinet minister, had a potentially top-class horse in his stable in the seventies. Border

Incident, after an impressive hurdling career, looked a likely future Gold Cup winner after his victory in the 1977 Embassy Final. Plagued by injury and a weak constitution, Border Incident did not appear in the Gold Cup until 1980. Ridden by John Francome he was to prove a disappointment. Sadly he never fulfilled his undoubted huge potential. If things had gone right for Border Incident, he could well have emulated his Rhonehurst predecessor Medoc II, who took the 1942 Gold Cup. His trainer later retired to his Wiltshire home and stewards at his local track, Salisbury, only a mile away. Richard Head, who is possessed of a tremendous sense of humour, once said he would have enjoyed his training career considerably more if he had not had to run his horses!

Nan Kennedy was a splendid character who trained at the now defunct College House stables in the village. Over the years she had a good horse every now and then. Hunting Cap, bred to win a 3-mile chase by Lord Leigh at Stoneleigh, won seven of the reel as a two-year-old. Pat Wilson held Mrs Kennedy's licence in those days. But it was in her own name she won the Schweppes with Ra Nova, later sold to Lord Matthews, at the end of her career. Until late in life she rode out with her tiny string. One day she brought a big ugly gelding to work with Peter Walwyn's string on the Faringdon Road gallop. Ridden by Walwyn's work rider Chris McNamee he beat some decent horses in the work. Those who saw the gallop invested profitably when Mrs Kennedy took the horse the many miles to the seaside track of Yarmouth. In the safe hands of Lester Piggott, Compound scored comfortably in a lowly selling race.

Another trainer in the village was the larger than life Ken Payne, who trained at Berkeley House in the early seventies. Payne, who was known universally as 'Window', gained the nickname as a result of his former profession as a window cleaner. Later, when he moved to Middleham in Yorkshire, he amassed a huge string, specializing in winning two-year-old sellers for the owners he reputedly found on endless visits to the clublands of the West End. One day he ran five horses in a seller at Doncaster. In the rush to saddle all his runners, an horrendous muddle occurred. Several of the horses running with the wrong saddles and consequently the wrong jockeys saw Payne severely reprimanded by the powers-that-be. In the end the logistics of training so many horses for so many owners became too much for Payne, his stable finally being dispersed after several of his owners complained that the horse they thought they owned was in fact running in somebody else's name.

In 1974 Simon Morant sold his Weathercock Stables, which he had originally bought from David Hastings, to Richard and Jenny Pitman. Morant, who had trained the good jumper Dan'l Widden and the sprint handicapper Parbleu was to start a new career as a Jockey Club starter, a position he maintains today. Richard and Jenny Pitman previously had lived at Hinton Parva where Jenny Pitman had held a licence. At the time Pitman was riding as first jockey for Fred Winter's Uplands yard. Mrs Pitman knew Upper Lambourn well as she had worked for Major Champneys at the yard, from where Nick Gaselee was to train the 1992 National winner Party Politics, some 200 yards down the road. The early years saw Jenny Pitman struggle to establish herself, even taking lodgers for the big flat stables in the village. In 1983 she became the first lady trainer to win the Grand National when the game little Corbiere jumped round Aintree like a buck in the hands of Ben de Haan. Corbiere attempted gallantly to add another National to his tally in the forthcoming years, but the handicapper never forgave him for the easy 1983 victory, the little horse being burdened with too much weight for ever more.

Corbiere gave Jenny Pitman the publicity she needed. The trainer capitalized in no uncertain terms. In 1984 the northern rider Phil Tuck drove the huge Burrough Hill Lad up the Cheltenham hill to bring a first Gold Cup to Weathercock House. Although Burrough Hill Lad was not entirely to fulfil his enormous potential in later years (a tendency to break blood vessels making him somewhat inconsistent), Mrs Pitman's stable went from strength to strength, the yard next door being purchased to accommodate her ever increasing string. In 1990 Toby Tobias was beaten by the slenderest margin in the Gold Cup, ridden by Jenny Pitman's son Mark. The next year the Pitmans gained ample compensation when the relatively unfancied Garrison Savannah beat the French raider The Fellow by a short head with the famous grey Desert Orchid fifteen lengths back in third.

Mrs Pitman's stable's rise to prominence in the eighties was not Lambourn's only success story. Fred Winter's former assistant Nicky Henderson bought the Windsor House establishment in the village of Lambourn and commenced training with three horses at the beginning of the 1975 season. One of his first successes was with the hurdler Main Ingredient, who was later to die tragically in a fire when lodging down the road at College House. A survivor of the fire was The Tsarevich, later to score at the Cheltenham Festival and run a splendid second in

Jenny Pitman with two favourite servants: Corbiere (white face) and Burrough Hill Lad

Maori Venture's National. It was the National of 1979 that saw the for-mer amateur rider attract the racing public's attention to his Lambourn yard. The former Tom Jones-trained Zongalero, brought skilfully back to his old form, finished a close second to the Scottish horse Rubstic in an exhilarating duel.

As Henderson's string increased the quality of horse improved. In 1984 before the Cheltenham meeting, the good flat horse See You Then arrived at Windsor House from Con Collins's Curragh stable, the

Triumph Hurdle as his target. Although he was only to run second in the four-year-old race, it was the start of an association with the Gloucestershire course for See You Then which was to prove increasingly productive. For the next three years he was to win the Champion Hurdle for Henderson's stable. His impressive surge of acceleration when Steve Smith Eccles pressed the button prompted older observers to rate him on a par with the great champions of yesteryear, Sir Ken and Hatton's Grace.

In his stable the great hurdler was very bad-tempered, his trainer never entering his box unless he was tied up. Like all true professionals he never settled into retirement. His fragile front legs recovered, he made an incredible comeback in the season of 1989-90. Though the will was there, the engine was not. He was retired again after running down the field to another useful former flat racer Kribensis.

The consistency of the Henderson stable's success at the major meetings saw his string become one of the largest in the land. A new yard was built behind the garden at Windsor House and Barry Hill's former second yard at Bourne House was bought when the South Bank trainer moved to Manton. Finally in 1992, at the end of the National Hunt season, Nick Henderson moved his huge jumping string to Peter Walwyn's former yard at Seven Barrows. With him he took what he believes to be the classiest steeplechaser he has ever handled – the 1992 Cheltenham two mile champion and Liverpool winner Remittance Man.

Henderson, who gave up a City career for the more perilous racing game, is by his own admission a bag of nerves before the big meetings. The spring of 1986 saw the east wind blow the whole of early March. Henderson, unable to sleep, spent the nights harrowing his all-weather ring on his tractor so that his Cheltenham horses could canter on a frost free surface the next morning. His wife Diana, a daughter of the late John Thorne of Spartan Missile fame, recalls that March as the only one in which she had, pre-Cheltenham, a good night's sleep.

In 1984 Oliver Sherwood, Henderson's successor as Fred Winter's assistant, bought the famous Rhonehurst establishment from Richard Head. A fine amateur rider, who had partnered his father's good chaser Venture to Cognac to many successes, Sherwood, as well as learning his trade from the fine trainer, contrived also to marry the boss's daughter, Denise. Sadly they are no longer together. In his early years at Rhonehurst, he had a fine prospect. The Breener, purchased from Arthur Moore's Irish yard, was a horse of the highest potential. He was to be

Sherwood's first winner. Tragically a fatal Cheltenham fall the year after was to bring the promising horse's career to an early close.

Sherwood quickly attracted some of jumping's major owners, notably Britain's highest earner, the banker, Christopher Heath. It was with Mrs Heath's The West Awake, ridden by his brother Simon, that Sherwood scored his first festival success in 1986 winning the Stayers Hurdle. The following year Sherwood won two races at the festival for Mrs Heath, The West Awake this time being joined on the roll of honour by Rebel Song. On the retirement of his brother Simon, Sherwood retained the young Yorkshireman, Jamie Osborne as first jockey. In 1992 Osborne was the leading rider at the Festival. Sherwood has much increased the stabling at Rhonehurst, one of Lambourn's most attractive yards. In 1986 he built a further thirty boxes in a paddock next to his house. One of Sherwood's best horses currently is the fine 2-mile chaser Young Snugfit. Strangely he started his career running in 5-furlong sprints for Mick Easterby's stable. He also trains the 1990 Hennessy winner Arctic Call, who has now found his old form with a vengeance, finishing second in the 1992 Whitbread.

The Sherwood brothers: Simon (left) and Oliver

A stone's throw from Sherwood's Rhonehurst yard are the Old Manor stables of Kim Bailey. Bought from the retired trainer Nick Vigors, Bailey had only moved from his previous quarters at East Ilsley a few months before when he won the National of 1990 with the American owner Mrs Duffy's Mr Frisk. Ridden at Aintree by the journalist Marcus Armytage, Mr Frisk proved not the easiest horse to train. Hating the confines of exercise with the string, he preferred to be led riderless by Bailey's wife Tracy on her hunter. The firm ground Mr Frisk revelled in was a feature of the 1990 spring. Mr Frisk took advantage by adding Sandown's Whitbread to his tally that same year.

Kim Bailey now has a formidable string. The high-class King's Fountain, one of the biggest horses in training, is an inmate of his yard, as is one of the tiniest, the 1992 Gold Cup third and subsequent National fourth Dockland's Express. Dockland's Express carried all before him in 1991, winning the Racing Post Chase at Kempton and the Whitbread.

If Dockland's Express was destined not to provide Lambourn with its seventh National since the war, the neighbouring stables of Nick Gaselee had that honour. The giant Party Politics, sold by his owner David Stoddart on the eve of the race for the huge sum of £80,000, provided the former amateur rider and *Evening Standard* journalist with the greatest success of his fifteen-year training career. A formidable training performance it was as well, the huge eighteen-hand gelding having previously had two operations to correct a wind infirmity. Gaselee's win provided a notable link with the village's famous steeplechasing past. He had been Fulke Walwyn's assistant for many years before branching out on his own. The master trainer, if he had lived to see it, would have been the first to offer his congratulations.

At East Ilsley Roddy Armytage had some good horses in his Nelson House stables. Father of Mr Frisk's National winning rider, Marcus, Armytage sold the Nelson House stables for building. In recent times he has trained a reduced string near Middleham in Yorkshire. His Barona started favourite for the 1976 National, having fallen the previous year. He could only finish fourth to Rag Trade. Barona preferred the Scottish equivalent, winning the Ayr race in 1975 and 1976, ridden by Paul Kellaway. Proud Tarquin was another inmate of the Ilsley yard. He won the Whitbread of 1972 only to lose the race later in the stewards' room.

Desert Orchid's rider Simon Sherwood chose East Ilsley to launch his training career, building sumptuous stables on the Compton side of the

The 1992 National winner, Party Politics, with his trainer, Nick Gaselee

village. His Summerdown establishment sent out two Cheltenham winners in 1992. The Triumph fell to Duke of Monmouth and Dusty Miller won the County Hurdle. The Sherwood stable enjoys the patronage of the composer Andrew Lloyd Webber and seems set to be a major jumping yard of the future.

If Fulke Walwyn ruled the roost in Lambourn in the immediate post-war period, George Beeby's Hamilton House stables in Compton regularly plundered the top jump prizes at this time. Beeby's chief patron was Lord Bicester. The big, strong, short-legged, bold jumping chaser was Lord Bicester's trademark. For many years this type was looked upon as the perfect steeplechasing sort. The big pale chestnut Silver Fame won the 1951 Gold Cup for Beeby's Compton stable. The victory was a second triumph for Beeby in the race, his Brendan's Nephew having scored in 1939. Ridden by that most stylish of riders, Martin Molony, the twelve-year-old won by the shortest of heads from Mr J.V. Rank's

Greenogue. Many spectators thought Greenogue had prevailed but Molony placed the chestnut's head in front 5 yards from the post. Another inmate of the stable was the fine chaser Finnure, who beat the triple Gold Cup winner Cottage Rake by half a length in the 1949 King George. Cottage Rake turned the tables in the 1950 Gold Cup, beating Lord Bicester's horse by ten lengths.

Beeby never won the National for Lord Bicester, Roimond finishing second in the 1949 race to the George Owen-trained Russian Hero. It was Owen who had ridden Beeby's Gold Cup winner, Brendan's Nephew in the first year of the war. Roimond was ridden by Dick Francis at Aintree. Later he was to partner the unluckiest National loser ever, the Queen Mother's Devon Loch. Later Beeby was to leave the jumping game, turning his attentions exclusively to the flat until his retirement in 1971.

Ken Cundell trained a large mixed string from Roden House. In 1966 he won the Hennessy with the Stan Mellor-ridden Stalbridge Colonist, beating Arkle, who gave the Compton horse 31 lb. Stalbridge Colonist later was to miss out narrowly winning a Gold Cup. In the 1967 race he was beaten by only three-quarters of a length by Woodland Venture. The following year he finished third to Fort Leney beaten by just over a length. Peter Cundell took over the stable in 1974 on his father's retirement. He soon had a top-class chaser at Roden House. In 1977 Peter Harris's Bachelor's Hall carried all before him in the early part of the season, winning the Mackeson, Hennessy and King George. After his long season he could not have benefited from the fact that the Gold Cup was abandoned in March. He finished fourth in the reopened event in April to Midnight Court. Another good chaser Cundell had in the late seventies was Peter Harris's Coolishall, only beaten two lengths in fourth when Lucius won the 1978 National. Coolishall contested the National several times, falling when a strong fancy in 1979. In 1982 Cundell had the misfortune to lose the fine hurdler Celtic Ryde. The winner of sixteen of his twenty-three races, he broke his neck when, an even money favourite, he fell for the first time in his career in Haydock's January Champion Hurdle trial. Nowadays few jumpers are trained in Compton. David Arbuthnot and Peter Cundell concentrate more on the flat.

Compton, though, was home to the shock 1967 National winner Foinavon. Trained at a small yard, which is no longer used for racing, just off the track which leads towards Fulke Johnson-Houghton's famous

Woodway gallops, Foinavon was the only horse to negotiate the carnage caused by the riderless Popham Down running down the fence after Becher's Brook. The leaders fell and every horse in contention was brought to a standstill. Only the 100–1 outsider, Foinavon, racing in the rear, was able to avoid the fracas. John Buckingham, taking Foinavon to the wide outside, jumped the fence safely and was gone beyond recall. Although Honey End tried gallantly to peg Foinavon's lead back, the Compton horse was fifteen lengths clear at the line. Foinavon's trainer John Kempton fancied his horse's chance so little that he preferred to go to Worcester to ride one of the stable's hurdlers, Three Dons. Three Dons was to win as well. Foinavon was formerly trained by Tom Dreaper and bought by Kempton for only 2,000 gns, having won only one of his twenty-two previous starts. Ridden by Kempton, he had finished tailed off in the Gold Cup behind Woodland Venture and appeared to have no chance at Aintree. Foinavon was brought down in the 1968 National, when he started at 66–1. His victory did not improve the fortunes of his small stable, his trainer leaving the ranks of his profession soon after.

There is some doubt as to where Foinavon concluded his Aintree preparation. Fulke Johnson-Houghton thinks his Woodway gallops can claim all the credit, although formal permission to use them was never granted. Early morning visits to Woodway, before the high-class flat racers left the warmth of their stables, were obviously most beneficial!

6
THE TRAINING GROUNDS OF THE BERKSHIRE DOWNS

The chalk downs which run along Berkshire's northern border are by their very constitution made for training the racehorse. In places the chalk runs to an incredible 700 ft deep. The free-draining aspect of the soil is perfect for the thoroughbred. Heavy falls of rain drain quickly through the chalk. Thus the thoroughbred trained on downland rarely encounters the heavy gluepot conditions which much rain produces in soils constituted of clay.

Before the Second World War the downland areas were agriculturally used exclusively by sheep. The shepherds would move the huge flocks around their area in a strict rota, ensuring that the downland grasses were cropped exactly to the right length. The early trainers could work hand in hand with the shepherd. Not only was his flock a most efficient form of early mowing machine, it was also a marvellous natural fertilizer. Carefully shepherded sheep can spread manure just as efficiently as modern machinery.

During the war a large area of the downs went under the plough. Later much ground was fenced, and the area gained its modern look. The early landowners realized that the crop yields on the chalk based soils were far less than on the more fertile valley plains. Before the advent of modern machinery and fertilizer, it was more economical for them to leave the downs to their sheep and the racehorses. Trainers made much use of the unfenced downland in the foothills, and there were endless canters over open ground. Far more grassland was available in the early days than it is now.

The centuries old sheep-farming tradition had an important consequence for the development of racehorse training on the Berkshire Downs. The area never went under the plough. As a result the gallops used by present-day trainers are in many cases untilled turf. Therein lies their excellence. The downland grasses mixed with herbs, only cropped by sheep before the advent of the mowing machine, have over the centuries formed a cushion-like texture, which even in the dryest of weather maintains a certain degree of 'give', never baking as the clay based soils of the valleys do. This unique free-draining sponge-like terrain is what has attracted horsemen to the downland areas since Cumberland sent his string of horses to be trained at Kate's Gore.

The Victorian trainer John Porter, who prepared a host of Classic winners at his Kingsclere stables in Hampshire described the benefits of the chalk downs for preparing the racehorse in his book *John Porter of Kingsclere*. What he wrote describes these benefits perfectly and definitely stands the test of time. Porter was a great advocate of his downland facilities and was rather scathing in his appreciation of the heathlands of Newmarket:

Newmarket is at a disadvantage in comparison with a down country, in as much as it is so level. Horses that climb up and down in their daily exercise develop all their muscles, because every one is brought into constant play in the ascent and descent of the hills. Again there is much more elasticity in the turf of old downland than there is in that of flat and more or less artificially preserved pasture. What with the large number of horses that are kept in work at Newmarket, and the unceasing rolling and bush-harrowing which have become necessary to the ground, all the 'life' is taken out of it. Downland, I may remark is very expensive to keep in order, because all tracks have to be put in by hand with 'rammers' and other appliances. In my own practice, I seldom resort or never resort to rolling the gallops after Christmas. They are all put in order at the end of the racing season, and the spring frosts breaking up the surface again, they remain good going the whole of the ensuing summer. Otherwise if you defer the operation of rolling the gallops until say February, and then get the March winds upon them, you have a hard surface, which remains so for the rest of the season. The proper management of the Downs requires careful attention on the part even of a trainer like myself, who has lived upon them all my life.

Because of the nature of the country they are set in, the training grounds of Berkshire necessitate a different type of training to that employed on the flatter heathland of Newmarket. The majority of Berkshire's training gallops are set so that horses are working up hill, or

Peter Walwyn's string cantering on the Faringdon Road gallops

on the collar from the start to the finish. The famous Faringdon Road gallops on the Wantage Road from Lambourn, where many Classic winners have been prepared, are a fine example. Though horses can only work a mile here, such is the severity of the climb from start to finish, that a certain degree of finesse is required in riding a gallop. If the gallop is conducted at too fast an early pace, the horse, however good, will have no reserves left to finish strongly. As a result the downland trainer need not work his horses as fast and as far as his Newmarket counterpart. The terrain of the downland will do much of the donkeywork for him, as John Porter so rightly described.

It is no accident that Berkshire has such a record in the jumping field. The nature of the gallops gives the delicate legs of the old steeplechaser far more chance to last longer. He can be brought to peak fitness by working in a far more collected fashion and at not so fast a pace as those prepared on flatter terrains. As Porter explains, the downland-trained horse is working all the time from the minute he leaves his stable. From the 1850s onward the downlands increased in popularity. It is of great relevance that at this time trainers became progressively less hard on their horses than their predecessors, realizing they did not need to be sweated and worked at full tilt over long distances to attain peak fitness. The clever ones let the natural aspects of the training grounds do it for them.

When Porter wrote at the turn of the century, training stables had fewer inmates than nowadays. Forty horses in a yard was a sizeable string at the turn of the century. Although John Scott had a hundred horses at Malton in the 1850s strings of this size were a rarity rather than the norm. Porter for instance had only fourteen horses in his first year training for Sir Joseph Hawley at Kingsclere in 1867. As Porter built on his success, and the stature and strength of his stable increased, so did those of his Berkshire counterparts. The area, capitalizing on the superb downland training facilities, quickly rose to the prominent position it holds to this day.

Lambourn started life centuries ago as a small market village. Not far below the Ridgeway, which straddles the Downs from Devizes in the west to Streatley near Reading in the east, the market was a natural development, as the old time drovers on their way to the large markets further east at Ilsley and Reading rested their flocks on the Ridgeway after their long journeys. As well as fulfilling the needs of the farmers nearby, the drovers, no doubt seeking an early return sold some of their stock there. The market declined and as the drovers' trade became increasingly redundant as transport and communications improved through the eighteenth and nineteenth centuries, Lambourn became famous for the horse.

As long ago as the 1840s, records relate that a certain William Ford trained horses in the High Street. When Wild Dayrell was resident at Ashdown for his Derby preparation, Joseph Saxon, who won the 1861 Oaks with Brown Duchess, was an established figure in the village. Harry Rodbourne, later to become a famous gallop tout in Lambourn, was attached to Saxon's stable as a jockey before his retirement in 1845. Prince was training at Seven Barrows two miles to the east, when Oates prepared Kettledrum to win the 1861 Derby.

By 1895 Charles Jousiffe, Surefoot's trainer at Seven Barrows, was dead and Garrett Moore was in the driving seat. James Chandler, who was to train Quintessence, Lambourn's next Classic winner, was at Lambourn House and James Humphreys at Lamborne Place behind the church. Harry Bates, son of the famous Middleham trainer Fred, was just commencing his career at Stork House. Strangley, these three training

Lamborne Place in the 1890s: the trainer, James Humphreys, is in the foreground mounted on his hack

establishments were featured in 1895 in an issue of the pictorial magazine of the day, *Racing Illustrated*. In the present day sadly only one is used for training. Lamborne Place was pulled down many years ago. Lambourn House, whose last incumbent was the Irishman Freddie Maxwell, was developed as housing after his retirement in the 1980s. Stork House is still used as a training stable although on a greatly reduced scale.

Although two of these principal Victorian training establishments are now redundant, the twentieth century was to see the number of training stables in the village grow. After the First World War, Lambourn developed from a village with a few racing yards dotted around its confines into the training centre it has become in the present day. This development was due in no small way to the arrival in the village in the first years of the war of Hugh Nugent, whose grandfather Sir Charles came to train in Lambourn in 1914.

Nugent, after taking over his grandfather's Windsor Cottage stables, which is now part of the famous Windsor House establishment in Lambourn High Street, saw the potential of the village and its neighbour,

The yard at Stork House, Lambourn, at the turn of the century

the hamlet of Upper Lambourn, as a centre for training. He describes in
his memoirs, *The Sir*, the purchase of Limes Farm (a 500-acre freehold in
between Upper Lambourn and Seven Barrows) in the 1930s and how he
laid out the gallops, which are the nucleus of those used by the majority
of the public stables, jumping and flat, in the present day.

In an illuminating passage he explains how he worked out the original
dimensions of the famous Mandown Bottom gallop used by all the good
jumpers trained in the village. Riding a Douglas motorcycle round in
ever increasing circles, he doubled up the galloping area which previously
had been used by Fred Pratt, the private trainer to Jimmy de Rothschild,
by attaching a long bale of twine to the centre spot and releasing the
twine 12 yards at a time until he reached the perimeter. By this method
Nugent created at least four more separate gallops of 12 yards wide and a
mile-and-a-quarter round.

In similar fashion he laid out a 7-furlong gallop with seven separate
strips, working on the principle of one gallop for every day of the week,
on the back of Mandown Hill, towards Upper Lambourn from Mandown Bottom. On Maddle Farm, some land to the west of Mandown, he
widened a mile gallop, which Pratt had also used, to make it four times
bigger. In addition he laid out six straight 5-furlong gallops 12 yards wide

and a left-handed mile-and-a-quarter gallop below the straight mile gallop on Maddle Farm. Although the Maddle Farm gallops, which incorporated a substantial schooling ground, were ploughed up after a dispute with the freeholder some twenty-five years ago, Nugent's son David, who by then was managing the gallops, made a new straight mile on the Mandown side by adding an extra furlong to the existing 7-furlong stretch. He also developed into galloping ground a 100-acre field above the Rhonehurst training establishment, to compensate for the loss of the excellent galloping facilities of Maddle Farm. Fulke Walwyn always believed that the Maddle Farm straight mile ground was superior to the ground on the newly appointed one on the Mandown side. A new schooling ground was designed at the bottom of the new straight mile to replace the old one at Maddle Farm. Sir Hugh with some justification, claimed that he doubted that anywhere else had a greater variety of galloping ground.

As well as developing the Mandown galloping area, Nugent was also responsible for improving and indeed starting some of the famous yards of today in their careers as racing establishments. Few stables were in Upper Lambourn in Nugent's early years. He recalled that only four trainers were resident in Upper Lambourn in 1914, the year of Sir Charles Nugent's arrival. Ralph Moreton, who had been John Porter's head lad at Kingsclere was resident at Park Farm, a half a mile beyond Upper Lambourn. He started training in 1905 after Porter's retirement. Fred Pratt, who had trained the 1911 1,000 Guineas winner Atmah at Letcombe Regis was at Waltham House, which is now the Lethornes training establishment. Pratt, who had also ridden a Guineas winner as a jockey, was a nephew of Fred Archer. At Saxon House, Ted Gwilt, who was to train Free Fare to win the Champion Hurdle, had already been ensconced for some years. Jimmy Rhodes was at Rhonehurst. He had come from his native Yorkshire to Lambourn to work for Garrett Moore at Seven Barrows in the 1890s, and was to train two Ascot Gold Cup winners in the twenties from this yard next to Saxon House.

Nugent purchased Rhonehurst on Rhodes's retirement and leased it to Reg Hobbs, Battleship's trainer, for the princely sum of 50*s* a week in the thirties. He designed a yard for Sir Victor Sassoon at Waldron Farm, which was to become the Berkeley House establishment in Upper Lambourn. He was also responsible for Uplands, Fred Winter's former yard, becoming a racing stable as well as Kingsdown where Peter Nelson was to send out the 1974 Derby winner, Snow Knight. He also increased the size of his grandfather's Windsor Cottage yard, which is now incorporated into the larger Windsor House establishment. From those early beginnings of half-a-dozen strings using Nugent's new facilities, in recent years there have been as many as twenty-three strings exercising on the Mandown Downs.

As well as the Mandown gallops, there are gallops on Neardown, across the valley from Mandown. To the west the famous Windmill Gallops climb steeply towards the village of Baydon and the M4 motorway. Windsor Lad was among the famous Lambourn winners prepared on this stretch of gallops. Freddie Maxwell trained the dual Ascot Gold Cup winner, Fighting Charlie, on these grounds as well as the fastest two-year-old of 1970, the filly Cawston's Pride. The Windmill gallops, well on the collar throughout their length, have been somewhat diminished in size since the golden days of Windsor Lad, due to encroachment by agriculture. However, it is still possible to work over a distance of ground round the valley left-handed, joining the straight at its outset. These gallops have been traditionally used by horses of trainers whose yards are based on the western side of the village, Windmill Hill being the gallops closest to their establishments. Since Dick Hern's move to Kingwood from West Ilsley, Windmill has been used exclusively by his string.

East of the village on the Wantage Road are the famous Faringdon Road gallops, which run steeply for 9 furlongs towards Wantage. On the left-hand side of the road travelling east are the gallops used by the powerful Lambourn yard of Barry Hills. On the right are those of the Seven Barrows establishment, from June 1992 occupied by Nick Henderson's jumping string and for twenty-five years previously by Peter Walwyn. These gallops are the oldest in the Lambourn area and over the years have been the scene for the preparation of many famous horses.

In 1911 Charles Morton, who trained eleven Classic winners for J.B. Joel from his Letcombe Regis, Oxfordshire yard conducted on the Faringdon Road gallops the best trial which he could recall in fifty years of training. Moreton placed his three-year-old colt Sunstar in a gallop with the high class old handicapper, Dean Swift; Spanish Prince, who was to win the Victoria Cup two weeks later; The Story, who was to carry a massive 10 st. 4 lb. to victory in the Prince of Wales Stakes at the Epsom Spring Meeting; and the three-year-old, Lycaon, who was to finish second in the St Leger of that year. Morton believed the gallop to offer

The Charles Morton-trained Sunstar winning the 1911 Derby. Sunstar did the best trial gallop Morton ever witnessed on the Faringdon Road working ground in the spring of 1911

the truest test for a class horse that he had ever experienced. In his own words, he described it as 'a particularly severe stretch of ground where it is all on the collar with no dip to give the horses a breather'.

Morton recalled his amazement when Sunstar appeared a furlong from the finish clear off his distinguished gallop mates, and maintained his advantage to the end. All the jockeys, who rode in that gallop on Good Friday 1911, assured Morton it was the finest trial they had ever ridden in. When The Story scored comfortably under his welterweight at Epsom ten days later, Morton knew he had the best three-year-old in England, as Sunstar had beaten The Story in a canter in the trial. His opinion was vindicated with Sunstar winning the 2,000 Guineas easily, and showing his class by winning the Derby when suffering from the lameness which was to bring his career to an end after his Epsom triumph.

All the Lambourn trainers used the Faringdon Road gallops in those early years. There are pictorial records of James Humphreys's string returning from work there in the year of 1895. Hugh Nugent recorded an example of their severity. His grandfather came back one day

James Humphreys's string at exercise on the Faringdon Road gallops, Lambourn in the 1890s

commenting that a newly arrived Letcombe trainer was letting his horses travel far too fast up the relentless climb. He predicted the unfortunate man would not last a year and his horses even less. According to Sir Hugh his grandfather was proved right, the Letcombe man going bust within a year. It is interesting that all Lambourn's post-war Classic winners have been prepared on the Faringdon Road gallops. Humble Duty, Polygamy and Grundy were trained by Peter Walwyn on the southern side. Snow Knight, from Peter Nelson's Kingsdown Upper Lambourn yard, was trained on the northern side, as were Barry Hills's two Guineas victors, Enstone Spark and Tap on Wood. Duncan Sasse, who trained the 1978 2,000 Guineas winner Roland Gardens, used a strip of gallop on the southern side beyond the Seven Barrows ground to prepare Roland Gardens for his win.

Further towards Wantage on the northern side of the road is the Moss Hill gallop, which much resembles the terrain and contours of Epsom racecourse. Peter Walwyn always used this gallop to give his Epsom Classic candidates experience of the gradients they would encounter on

Grundy (nearest) – his last gallop before the Derby

the big day. Grundy galloped on Moss Hill before his 1975 triumph.

Lambourn's development as a centre was a direct result of Hugh Nugent's decision to purchase Limes Farm between the wars. Trainers were able to pay per horse to use the facilities, in similar fashion to the Heath charges administered to trainers by the Jockey Club at Newmarket. Nugent's development of the facilities on Mandown encouraged the village as a centre for jumping. Until then the area had had a predominantly flat orientated outlook. Windmill and Faringdon Road gallops were what the professionals term 'summer ground', the preserve of the flat racer.

The famous gallops at Whatcombe on Woolley Down climb to their apex high above the Wantage/Newbury road. Leased from the Wroughton family of Woolley Park, five Derby winners have been prepared on this exclusive turf: Trigo and Blenheim by Dick Dawson in between the wars, Blakeney by Arthur Budgett in 1969 and his half brother Morston in 1973. Most recently Paul Cole won in 1991 with Fahd Salman's Generous. Working right-handed from a cottage on Woolley Park the mile-and-a-quarter gallop swings right-handed to join the steep straight, which rises on the collar to its culmination high above the road. Longer distances can be worked by initially working in circular fashion round the eastern side of the gallop and then joining the finishing straight. Arthur Budgett used this gallop to prepare Random Shot, his good long distance stayer of the early 1970s.

Also available to the master of Whatcombe is a gallop on Summer Down above Eastbury, on which Lord Stalbridge's famous jumpers were prepared in the 1940s. This gallop provides excellent ground in the spring before Woolley is open, and has a straight uphill 6 furlongs as a notable conditioning feature. Further cantering ground is available for spring and winter work in a large field opposite the entrance to the training place itself. The extensive training areas on Woolley Down incorporate gallops of all distances, which culminate in stiff uphill climbs. In downland fashion, even in their most basic work the horses are encountering muscle-building gradients from the second they leave the shelter of their boxes, whichever one of the varied training grounds is their destination. Whatcombe is one of the most exclusive private stables in the country. Its record in producing top-class horses throughout the years proves the point definitively.

At West Ilsley the training facilities are if possible even more complete than at Whatcombe. The famous summer gallops, which climb from the western end of the village towards the Ridgeway track in the direction of the Harwell Research complex are the *pièce de résistance*. A maze of beautifully maintained stretches of ground weave their way through the scrub and gorse. A famous trial ground runs from the tiny road that crosses the Ridgeway above Chilton Bottom a mile-and-a-quarter towards Scutchamer Knob, a small wood to the west. Famous names have completed their preparation for the great races on this trial ground. Brigadier Gerard beat Mill Reef in the memorable 1971 2,000 Guineas without the benefit of a racecourse outing. A fine gallop on the trial ground ensured he went to Newmarket at the peak of his fitness. Dick Hern, who trained legions of top-class thoroughbreds on these grounds during his long tenure at West Ilsley, consistently produced his charges fit to win in the highest of classes without the benefit of a run. The Queen's Highclere, who won the 1974 1,000 Guineas and Nashwan's legendary 2,000 win of 1989 are notable examples.

The summer gallops are never used at West Ilsley if the ground is riding soft. Over the years this practice has ensured the ground remains like a billiard table, never cut to ribbons in rain-sodden heavy conditions. Some years ago Hern had a Derby candidate, Admiral's Launch, who subsequently proved a disappointment. Leaving nothing to chance in his preparation, Hern installed mats at intervals on one of the summer gallops to prepare his animal for the road crossings on the Derby course. Eddie Reavey, who trained next door at East Hendred until his death in 1980, used to say that he could never understand why they were called the summer gallops: they were just as good in the spring. Reputedly Reavey, who specialized in preparing fast early two-year-olds made a clandestine visit or two to the hallowed summer ground in the spring, if he had a promising early sort!

Christopher Loyd, whose family has owned these famous summer downs for many years, recalls riding his pony as a child alongside the trial ground in the summer of 1935. He came across the famous jockey Freddie Fox in urgent conversation with Captain Gooch, the West Ilsley trainer of the day, about some recent gallop. Fox declared that if he could not ride Barham in the Derby, he would definitely choose the small pony. Loyd remembers in the flushes of his youth believing the great jockey and rushing hotfoot home to report to his family. Fox was to supplement his Guineas win on the great Barham with a Derby victory. Only a fall in a selling race at Doncaster the day before the St Leger prevented him from riding Barham in the final stage of his triple crown triumph.

Ploughed up during the war was the famous Lord Lyon gallop, where James Dover is reputed to have prepared the Triple Crown winner of 1866. Starting on the Rowstock side of the Harwell Research centre, the gallop wound its way above Chilton Bottom to end up on the Ridgeway in the vicinity of the West Ilsley summer ground. A stiff test it must have been as it climbed steeply to its end. William Stevens brought Merry Hampton to work there from Compton in 1887 before his subsequent removal to Newmarket two weeks before his Epsom win.

For spring work and cantering ground Hodcott House uses gallops on the East Ilsley side of the village. Uphill from start to finish they climb in a slight left-handed curve towards the summit on the top of Gore Hill and the Oxford/Newbury road. The stretch of ground on the East Ilsley side, known as Gilberts, is notoriously severe. Willie Carson, for many years Hern's stable jockey at Ilsley, described Gilberts as 'soon sorting out the men from the boys'. It is only a decent animal that travels strongly in the final stages of a gallop on this ground. The superb heavily muscled athletes, which were Hern's trademark during his time at Hodcott, did all their early conditioning work on this ground.

East Ilsley trainers of recent years have used Fulke Johnson-Houghton's famous gallops above Blewbury for grass work, coupled with the Churn gallops, until recently leased from Reading University and managed by the Woodway trainer, and the Compton gallops of the Cundell family. The grass gallops on Gore Hill, on the East Ilsley side of the main road, are now used for sheep farming. A famous gallop on the Churn estate, the Pennings, climbs steeply from the old Compton/Upton railway line to circumnavigate a prominent wood at its summit. Jumping trainers rate this gallop highly as a test for their charges. The Woodway gallops are also rich in their variety since the inclusion of ground previously used by Frank Cundell, the Aston Tirrold trainer. This acquisition more than compensated Johnson-Houghton for the loss of the Churn gallops.

The gallops on Compton and Roden Down owned by Ken Cundell, a cousin of Frank, are excellent for steeplechasers and flat horses alike. Situated on the opposite side of the old railway from the Churn gallops, the ground climbs on the collar in circular fashion towards the Ridgeway. It is possible to work as far as 1 mile 3 furlongs here. Alternatively trainers have the option of working 5 furlongs back towards Compton village uphill on a stretch of ground known as Oxford Hill. An extensive school-ing ground and a 4-furlong stretch exist in what is called the Jumping Field by the railway line. Steeplechasers such as Bachelor's Hall, Stal-bridge Colonist and Celtic Ryde can be prepared as easily as top-class sprinters, such as March Past and King of Spain, on the Compton gallops. In the dry spring of 1991 many of the Lambourn jump trainers took their Cheltenham hopes to gallop on the Compton ground. The number of horses prepared at Compton is much less than in the 1950s and '60s, when Ken Cundell handled a large mixed string, and consequently the best ground has been used sparingly and is relatively fresh.

As John Porter wrote, much care is needed in the maintenance of gal-lops. Economics and the larger strings of present-day trainers preclude in many cases the putting back of gallops by hand. Porter's dreaded harrow is far more in evidence these days. The famous trial ground at West Ilsley, however, is always forked back. Basically the less heavy machinery that is present on a gallop the better it will ride. Present-day trainers have many modern inventions to aid the preparation of their charges.

The invention of the all-weather gallop, a child of the sixties, has been a boon in this respect. Usually wide enough to accommodate and enable two horses to work together upsides, the gallop consists of an artificial surface of wood, rubber, treated ash or sand. Dug deep to allow perfect drainage, a most important feature, a membrane is placed below the surface to stop stones or flints rising. Whichever artificial surface is preferred is then added. The advantage of these artificial gallops is twofold. In dry weather routine work can be continued avoiding the injuries that firm ground can bring to the fragile legs of the thoroughbred. Conversely, in very wet conditions the modern trainer, in many cases with far larger strings than his predecessors, can save his valuable turf from the inevitable damage that continued use in inclement weather brings.

All-weather gallops are now a feature of every training place in Berkshire. The modern trainer cannot compete without one. The contours of the downland are the perfect location for all-weather gallops. The most successful ones climb from their beginning to end. Built on the collar they tend to ride much better. Set on the chalk they also drain quickly, a most important factor if the surface is to remain constant and true. Whatcombe has a most successful woodchip version in the paddock close to the yard. On Faringdon Road Peter Walwyn had one of the first shavings gallops in the late sixties. He has most recently built one of the rubber variety. Other successful artificial surfaces are two types built on the West Ilsley winter ground. There is one of Equitrack and one of woodchip. Both climb in the recommended way through their length. Simon Sherwood has recently totally renovated the East Ilsley all-weather gallop most successfully. Barry Hills prefers the shavings variety on his Faringdon Road gallops, but now uses woodchips, as shavings have become very difficult to obtain. It is the individual trainer's choice as to what surface he employs. One thing is certain. These gallops are expensive to install and to maintain: the surfaces tend to break up with the harrowing and the rolling required to keep them in order. Essentially they are the most important feature of the modern training place. Martin Pipe, the most successful jumping trainer ever, uses nothing else at his Wellington, Somerset, base.

The modern-day racehorse tends to exercise for less time than his ancestors. Economics are as much the cause as anything else. The stable-lad of years ago rode two horses only at exercise a day: his present-day counterpart rides three or often four. As a result the old-fashioned trainer had his horses out for much longer daily exercise. Charles Morton used to have his horses led by their riders to the Faringdon Road gallops over three miles away from his Letcombe Regis yard, and led back again after they had galloped. Ken Cundell remembers in the fifties bringing horses to work at Chilton, a considerable distance away, just as his nineteenth-century predecessor William Stevens had done.

Nowadays the fact that horses travel in highly sophisticated boxes is almost taken for granted. In the early days horses were walked to their racecourse destination, journeys that could often take many days. Later horse vans, such as the one used to transport Wild Dayrell to Epsom in 1855 were used. These vans were pulled by coach horses and must have been an uncomfortable and stuffy conveyance. By the 1840s, as a result of the Industrial Revolution, railways sprung up around the country. The branch lines which followed in the ensuing years proved to be of great benefit to the racing fraternity. In 1898 a branch line was opened between Lambourn and Newbury and the railway had reached Compton earlier. Trainers were able to transport their charges all over the country making use of the ever increasing railway network. Although horses had been transported by rail from major stations before this, it was a great bonus to trainers when their horses could board the trains nearer home, avoiding the long walks on dusty roads. Carriages with special horse stalls were at first attached to regular services, but as the service became increasingly popular special horse transport trains were run, the trainers booking a stall for their charges. There is no doubt that the Great Western Railway extension made Berkshire more accessible to the outside world. It is no accident that her racehorse population increased hand in hand with the development of the railway.

As the motorized horse box developed between the wars, the railway was destined to decline in time. Horses, however, travelled by train until after the Second World War. Older residents of the Berkshire training villages can still remember the flickering lamps and the sharp beat of the horses' hooves as the runners made their way back along the country roads from the tations to their stable yards late at night. Hugh Nugent with a Letcombe operator Mervyn Scott, saw the potential of the motorized horse box in the thirties. Soon he had developed a formidable fleet used by all the local trainers. It was Nugent's Lambourn Transport boxes that moved Harry Cottrill's horses to safety from the 1937 fire, which devastated Seven Barrows. Nowadays many individual trainers prefer to have their own horse

Three Victorian Lambourn trainers with other local worthies. James Humphreys is seated on the left of the vicar. Standing on the vicar's left is Harry Bates; standing on his right is James Chandler

boxes. The monopoly of the large firms has consequently declined.

An interesting example of the distances which the old trainers were prepared to travel their horses to find suitable trial tackle or suitable galloping ground, is afforded by a report in the *Sporting Gazette* of 1866, the year the East Ilsley-trained Lord Lyon won the triple crown. The paper's tout had been sent to Russley Park to chart the progress of Mat Dawson's Student, the winter favourite for the 1866 Derby. His life would not have been worth living if his presence had been detected by the great trainer. In those days trials and stable business were matters of great secrecy, especially as Dawson's patron at Russley, James Merry, was a gambler of considerable reputation. Undetected he was able to file a startling report, as follows:

Friday: The horses came out at ten past five that morning, accompanied by Mr Merry, Mat Dawson and Arthur Edwards, and walked under the plantation for a good half hour, but neither Student, Primate, Beelzebub, Zambesi, nor Watchbox were among them. Mr Dawson did nothing there, but proceeded direct to the White Horse Hill, nearly three miles further on, so you may fancy what a bucketting I had; and when I got there it was all over, so I can tell you nothing of the trial. One thing I am certain of, there was a stranger in it, and from what I could make out in the distance I'm pretty sure it was Lord Lyon. Mr Dover was trotting on his pony alongside of him — that I'm sure of, as I could swear to him a mile off by his elbows; and the man on the horse was very like Custance, only he had a light beard — a disguise perhaps.

The gallop on that April Friday must have answered some questions. Lord Lyon was to win all three Classics, and Student was to prove an unworthy Derby favourite. Dover and Dawson were happy to find out the merits of their Classic hopes in a highly secretive trial. The bookmakers presumably suffered considerably as Lord Lyon was an odds-on favourite for all three of his Classic victories. He had travelled nearly twenty miles from his East Ilsley base to take part in the trial high above Lambourn on what are now Henry Candy's gallops on White Horse Hill. For many years touts were the only source of information that the bookmakers and the sporting press had with regard to gallops. In those days horses had to be confirmed as runners on the actual raceday. Trainers delighted in deceiving the touts over the destination and targets of their stable inmates. It was only when overnight declaration of runners was made compulsory that the newspapers were able to print accurate lists of runners. When this reform occurred, the role of the tout became redundant.

For many years the Rodbourne family, descendants of the same Harry who rode for Joseph Saxon in the 1840s, reported on the gallops for the racing press in the Lambourn area. Hugh Nugent recalled with relish how a stablehand of his, walking the good hurdler Song of Essex swathed in bandages, persuaded the Rodbourne of the day that the horse was injured and would not fulfil his engagement the next day. Rodbourne swallowed the tall story and informed the press that Song of Essex would not run. The horse, who was one of the best hurdlers of the early 1930s, ran and finished second to Dorothy Paget's Insurance in the Champion Hurdle the next day, landing Nugent some large each way bets struck in the morning. The bookmakers accepted large sums at ridiculously long prices as they were sure the animal was tucked up safely in his home stable!

The old chalk downland was the original reason why the racehorse came to Berkshire. Modern technology has presented the trainer of today with many aids his predecessors did not have. All-weather gallops, motorized horse boxes, electrically powered hot walking machines and heated swimming pools would not have been imagined by James Dover in his wildest dreams. He would have known, though, that no famous racehorse would have been sent to be trained in Berkshire if it was not for the county's most ancient and most durable asset in racing terms, its natural exercise grounds high on the windswept downs. They are the catalyst of Berkshire's development as a premier training area over the last 150 years.

7
THE ROYAL CONNECTION

The 1960s saw the training grounds of Berkshire stamped with the seal of royal approval. Although Norah Wilmot had from time to time had the odd horse for the Queen and the Queen Mother at her stables near Bracknell at Binfield Grove, not since the days of the Duke of Cumberland in the eighteenth century had the royal family's bloodstock been trained in substantial numbers within the county's boundaries. In the winter of 1966 six of the Queen's yearlings arrived at the West Ilsley yard of Dick Hern, only a mile from the old Cumberland stables at Kate's Gore. In 1973 the Queen Mother's string of jumpers was to move from Kent, after the death of her trainer Peter Cazalet, to the Saxon House stables of Fulke Walwyn in Upper Lambourn.

Hewett, the Berkshire chronicler, told how George IV, when still Prince Regent, expressed a desire to lease the Cumberland stables at Kate's Gore on his uncle's death. The owner, though, displeased by the behaviour of the Duke's stable staff, pulled the stables to the ground. The foundations of the famous stables at Kate's Gore are still visible on the left of the A34, going south, as the road climbs steeply to the summit of Gore Hill. Overgrown now with grass, the curious stepped formations rising towards the Ridgeway are where those great racehorses, Herod and Eclipse, reputedly were housed in their early years. The Prince Regent did not pursue his interest in the Kate's Gore establishment and had his horses trained in Newmarket for the rest of his life. His principal achievement on the turf was when he won the Derby of 1788 with the odds-on favourite Sir Thomas, trained by the leading Newmarket handler Frederick Neale, who won six Derbys in a long career.

Edward VII, when Prince of Wales, first had his horses trained at Kingsclere by John Porter. A string of moderate animals was the feature of Porter's time as trainer to the Prince of Wales. After a few years the royal string was moved to the Newmarket yard of Richard Marsh. The Egerton House trainer was most successful for his royal patron, winning the Derby of 1896 with Persimmon and the triple crown with Diamond

Jubilee in 1900. Marsh also won the king his only Classic as monarch when Minoru won the Derby by a head from Louviers in the hands of Herbert Jones in 1909. Tumultuous cheers and celebration occurred on Epsom Downs after the King's triumph. Before the next Derby was run, Edward VII was dead.

George V continued to have his horses trained by Marsh although without the success of his father. In 1914 the King won the Middle Park with the fast two-year-old Friar Marcus. Two successive Royal Hunt Cups with Weathervane were the highlight of the later years. At the end of the 1924 season Richard Marsh retired, and the royal string was taken over by William Rose Jarvis, the brother of Jack and Basil Jarvis and grandfather of the William Jarvis who trains in Newmarket now.

In 1928 William Jarvis won George V the 1,000 Guineas with Scuttle, ridden by Joe Childs. This was to be the only Classic winner to carry the royal colours during the King's reign. In 1942 the Egerton House estate was sold and broken up. William Jarvis, by then a sick man, retired from training. He died in the January of 1943. Cecil Boyd-Rochfort was appointed as King George VI's trainer at Newmarket, and trained the horses bred at the royal stud. Those animals leased to the King by the National Stud were trained at Beckhampton by the master of his profession Fred Darling. As it was a commercial enterprise the National Stud leased its animals for their racing careers originally to Lord Lonsdale. Later the lease was taken over by George VI. On his death in 1952 the lease was continued by the present Queen but this practice stopped in the 1960s when the stud ceased to be a breeding establishment. Darling was most successful for the King, winning the 1942 2,000 with Big Game and the fillies' triple crown with Sun Chariot the same year. The royal stud at Sandringham's fortune was also on the rise. Boyd-Rochfort won the 1946 1,000 Guineas with Hypericum, the last Classic winner the King was to own.

The present Queen inherited her father's racing interests on her accession in 1952. In 1947 Fred Darling had retired. Noel Murless had moved from Yorkshire to Beckhampton, inheriting the leased royal horses from Darling. In the autumn of 1952 Murless left Beckhampton for Newmarket, taking the new Queen's horses with him. The downlands of the southern counties were to lose the royal horses for more than a decade. Newmarket was to benefit considerably. In 1953 Captain Boyd-Rochfort saddled Aureole to finish second in the Derby to Pinza. After finishing a disappointing third in the St Leger, he stayed in training at four. Having won the Hardwicke narrowly at Royal Ascot, his final race was to be his best. Ridden by Eph Smith, he won the King George VI and Queen Elizabeth Stakes for his young owner Queen Elizabeth. Aureole could not have chosen a more apt event in which to run his finest race, as George VI had bred him. The Queen did not have to wait long for her first Classic. In 1957 Lester Piggott steered the filly Carozza, leased by the Queen from the National Stud and trained by Noel Murless, to victory in the Oaks. Boyd-Rochfort was not long in mirroring Murless's success. The very next year Pall Mall won the 2,000 Guineas for the Queen, ridden by Doug Smith. Pall Mall was the stable's second string: Harry Carr, the stable jockey, chose to partner Bald Eagle.

Strangely Murless and Boyd-Rochfort were not to win another British Classic winner for their Queen. Although Cecil Boyd-Rochfort was to saddle many winners in the royal colours until his retirement in 1968, no horse of the quality of Aureole was to emerge from the royal stud during the Captain's career. Canisbay who won the Eclipse in 1965 was the best royal horse Boyd-Rochfort had in the twilight of his time as a trainer. He also won the Goodwood Cup in two successive years for the Queen in the sixties, with Apprentice and Gaulois. Murless trained the high-class stayer Hopeful Venture, one of the last horses bred at the National Stud, for the Queen. Second in the St Leger he had a wonderful four-year-old season, winning the Ormonde, the Hardwicke and the Grand Prix de Saint Cloud in 1968.

The inevitable fact that Boyd-Rochfort would soon retire was the catalyst for a royal return to Kingsclere. In December 1963 Peter Hastings-Bass took delivery of his first batch of the Queen's yearlings. In April 1964 he saddled his first and only winner in the royal colours when Planta Genista won at Lingfield. In June 1974 Hastings-Bass died at only forty-four years of age. His assistant Ian Balding, who later married Emma, Hastings-Bass's daughter, took over the licence aged only twenty-six. The royal horses are still in his charge at Kingsclere. Peter Hastings-Bass's young son, William, aged only sixteen when his father died, is now the Queen's trainer at Hodcott House, West Ilsley. He is now known as Lord Huntingdon, having inherited that title recently. Thus as long ago as 1963 the royal connection with the Hastings-Bass family was forged.

At the end of 1966 Dick Hern received his first batch of royal yearlings. One of these was St Patrick's Blue, who was to win the 1970

Timeform Gold Trophy at Redcar. The royal link with the Berkshire training grounds was re-established. The link was to become stronger in the ensuing years. In 1970 Lord Porchester, a longtime confidante of the Queen, was appointed her racing manager, succeeding Richard Shelley. A year previously Porchester had suggested that the Queen should send her mare Highest to be covered by Queen's Hussar, whom his father had owned as a racehorse and stood at the family stud at Highclere, south of Newbury. The result of the 1970 mating was a good looking filly, later named Highclere after the place where she was conceived.

In the winter of 1972 Highclere was sent to Hodcott House to be trained. She had three outings only as a two-year-old, winning the Donnington at Newbury on her final start. She was given only 7 st. 11 lb. in the Free Handicap, the handicapper presumably thinking she would not be up to Classic standard. The handicapper could hardly have been more wrong.

Ridden by Joe Mercer, on her first outing of the season she beat the subsequent Oaks winner Polygamy by a narrow margin in the 1,000 Guineas, to give the Queen her first English Classic victory since Pall Mall won the 1958 2,000 Guineas. Highclere improved to take the Prix Diane at Chantilly on her next outing decisively. Upped in distance she next contested the King George VI at Ascot, running a fine race to finish second to Dahlia. She never showed that form again. However, her stud career which was to follow would have lasting consequences with regard to the royal racing fortunes.

The Queen's Silver Jubilee Year of 1977 saw Dunfermline, a filly by Royal Palace out of Strathcona, win the Oaks and the St Leger for Hern and his new stable jockey Willie Carson. Strangely Strathcona, although ten years old, was sold in foal to Town Crier at the 1976 December Sales for only 7,400 gns. Although Dunfermline had not won in 1976, she had finished second to Triple First in the May Hill Stakes at Doncaster and was also second in an Ascot group race. The decision to let Strathcona go so cheaply was strange, for Dunfermline turned into a filly of the highest class. Her strongest suit was stamina. There is no doubt she outstayed Alleged in the last few strides to record her Leger win, but Alleged turned the tables in the Arc de Triomphe. A slow early gallop did not suit the filly. She finished very strongly nearly grabbing third place on the line. The shorter distance of the Arc combined with the slow gallop is probably what beat her. She ran as a four-year-old, finishing second in the Hardwicke. Failing to find her three-year-old form, she was then retired to stud.

Dunfermline was the best filly that the Queen has bred to date. She was also the last Classic winner that the Queen has bred up to the present day. Her distinguished predecessor, Highclere's first foal Milford, arrived in Hern's yard in the autumn of 1978 to be broken. Second in the two races of his juvenile year, he looked a promising sort, especially as his mother had improved considerably from two to three. Two easy wins in the White Rose at Ascot and the Lingfield Derby Trial found the stable jockey Carson not sure if he would ride Milford at Epsom or the other Hodcott representative, Troy. History relates that in the end Carson chose right and plumped for Troy. Lester Piggott was engaged for Milford and the royal colt was a strong fancy to give the Queen an excellent Derby run. He ran a disappointing tenth to Troy. Back at Hodcott, it was decided to aim him at the St Leger.

At the Newmarket July meeting, he beat the useful M-Lolshan in the Princess of Wales. By the time of his next outing he was the St Leger favourite. Starting at odds-on for York's Great Voltigeur, he was a poor third to Noble Saint. Sent to Doncaster he was equipped with blinkers in the Leger. They did not help, Milford finishing tenth. In the autumn he was sold for a reputed £^{3}/$_4$ m. to stand at Lord Harrington's Greenmount stud. Milford was not the last of his mother's progeny to be sold for a great sum. Although found wanting in his major tests, Milford, by Derby winner Mill Reef out of a 1,000 Guineas winner, could hardly have been better bred.

Highclere's fourth foal, by Dick Hern's Leger winner Bustino, was born in 1979. Named Height of Fashion, she had a very good two-year-old career. First time out she won the Acomb at York, coincidentally the first race her sire Bustino ever won. Her next race was the May Hill at Doncaster, where she beat the useful Clare Island by a length. At Ascot in October the filly appeared to paddock judges to have thrived. She confirmed the impression by holding off Zinzara to score by half a length. As her sire and dam were late developers, she looked likely to be a major factor in the staying fillies' races at the age of three.

Although the winter favourite for the Oaks, Height of Fashion's first run of the season saw her fail to act on the gradients of Goodwood. She never appeared to be on an even keel. At one stage it looked unlikely she would pass her pacemaker Round Tower. It was announced after her unimpressive win that she would miss the Oaks at Epsom, her connections, on the evidence of the Goodwood race, feeling she was too big a filly to act. Her next race was the Princess of Wales at Newmarket, a more suitable terrain altogether. Equipped with blinkers to make Carson's job easier, she disposed of Amyndas with ease. The great stayer Ardross, over a trip patently too short for him, struggled in her wake.

Shortly after the race it was announced that Sheik Hamdan al Maktoum had paid in the region of £$1^1/_2$ m. for Height of Fashion, wishing to buy into the famous royal bloodline. Height of Fashion's two subsequent efforts on the racecourse made the purchase look expensive. After dwelling at the start, she never got into the race in the King George at Ascot. In the Yorkshire Oaks, her final start, she was last behind Awaasif. The huge filly was then retired to stud.

Far from being expensive, Height of Fashion proved to be the best investment Hamdan al Maktoum ever made. Her first foal by Northern Dancer was the high class stayer Alwasmi, who won the John Porter at Newbury. Sent to Northern Dancer again she produced Unfuwain. In 1988 Unfuwain proved to be among the best of his age. He won the Warren at Epsom in the spring by a wide margin. Subsequent wins in the Chester Vase and the Princess of Wales persuaded Dick Hern to let him take his chance against the older horses in the King George at Ascot. He ran a marvellous race to finish second to Mtoto. On his last outing of the season he ran a gallant fourth in the Arc to Tony Bin. In 1989 Unfuwain won the John Porter and the Jockey Club Stakes. The firm ground that prevailed that summer saw him retired early to stud, Dick Hern feeling he could not prepare Unfuwain satisfactorily at home.

If Unfuwain was top class, Height of Fashion's third foal was to prove the best. Covered this time by Blushing Groom, the high-class French miler, she was to produce Nashwan, the best racehorse Dick Hern says he ever trained. Carrying all before him, he won the 2,000, the Derby, the Eclipse and the King George in that golden summer of 1989. Blessed with stamina and speed in quantities that the great champions alone possess, Nashwan was to prove one of the best thoroughbreds ever to race in England.

The decision to sell Height of Fashion has been criticized in many quarters since. With hindsight it was disastrous in that it cost the Queen the chance to own a Derby winner. Even if she had not produced Nashwan, Height of Fashion was a major loss to the royal stud. Unfuwain was a far classier colt than any the Queen has owned in recent years. Height of Fashion had proved she could produce the goods consistently: the stallion seemed immaterial. This is the most important asset in a mare. From a commercial point of view, the decision has cost royal racing interests far more than the figure Sheik Hamdan paid in the summer of 1982. The royal studs have not produced an animal remotely close in class to Height of Fashion's first three foals. Unknown Quantity, who gave the Queen her first American victory in the August of Nashwan's Derby year at Arlington Park, Chicago, is probably the best to date. Lord Huntingdon and Ian Balding, the other royal trainer, have not in recent times received a top-class horse from Sandringham.

Of course there were mitigating circumstances. At the time the royal stud possessed no less than five mares out of Highlight, Height of Fashion's granddam, including her dam, Highclere. They also had at Sandringham a full sister to Height of Fashion, Beacon Hill. Height of Fashion's three-year-old career had proved a disappointment. She looked a likely Classic winner in the autumn of 1981. As an individual, the filly had grown lengthier and lighter throughout her three-year-old career. *Timeform* of 1982 were even moved to describe her as 'a plain Jane'. With what was to turn out as their greatest ever understatement, their contributor signed off: 'It will be interesting to see how she fares at stud.' Presumably the royal advisors patted themselves on the back as they banked the Arab prince's cheque.

They had plans to spend the money. In what subsequently was to be put forward as another reason for the sale of Height of Fashion, the Queen purchased the Hodcott House stables from the Weinstock family: the famous stables now had a royal owner. In the autumn of 1982 the incumbent trainer Dick Hern signed a seven-year lease which was to expire at the end of the 1989 flat season.

It was the Queen's decision not to renew Hern's lease that was to create a storm in racing circles. Criticism of the royal decision was unprecedented. The background is worth recapping. Having learnt to live with the partial paralysis from his 1984 hunting accident, the summer of 1988 saw Hern hospitalized for a serious heart operation. Neil Graham rushed back from America early, and it was announced that he would hold the licence until Hern was well enough to resume. The speed of Hern's recovery was unbelievable. Far from weakening the trainer, it appeared to galvanize him. He could not wait to be back at Hodcott at the helm. By 14 March

1989, when the Palace announced that Hern's lease would not be renewed and William Hastings-Bass would be appointed trainer in his place, Hern, fortified by a holiday in Dubai, was recovered and feeling better than he had for some time. He was in full control of the most promising bunch of horses, Nashwan included, he had had at West Ilsley for some time.

The racing press had a field day. Their criticism of the royal decision was unanimous. It was not so much the decision to replace Hern that rankled. After all, the Queen as owner of the stables was entitled to appoint who she liked as her trainer. It was more the undiplomatic and harsh manner in which it was handled that caused the ensuing furore. The bland statement without explanation in typical Palace fashion was seen to be callous. Hern had served the royal interests well in a loyal career and had proved that he could still maintain his high training standards, even when a very sick man. Proof positive was the stable's success at the end of the 1988 season when Hern masterminded the preparation of the Leger winner Minster Son from his hospital bed.

The criticism did not make the Palace react in the slightest. Hern himself typically refused to comment, although he was left, in the wake of the Palace decision, with effectively nowhere to go when the 1989 season ended. Willie Carson, Hern's stable jockey was more forthright. Criticizing the decision in no uncertain terms, he commented: 'The Major has come a long way through a very dark tunnel since his accident and now, just when we were beginning to see the light, it's as though someone had dropped a trapdoor and shut off that light.'

The Palace's decision had been made some time before the March announcement. The process was discussed and put in motion when Hern was at his lowest ebb during his illness in 1988. There is little doubt that the Palace was caught on the hop by Hern's rapid and miraculous recovery, but the fact remains that it made no difference. The decision was final, although the reasoning behind it was less clear. Since his hunting accident, Hern had proved he could continue to produce the goods. Further adversity, in the guise of his serious heart problem and subsequent operation, had not stopped him either. If the Palace thought Hern was not the trainer that he had been, he could not have rebutted this assumption more completely. Within six weeks of the announcement he was to produce his finest training performance when Nashwan was produced as fit as a fiddle on the day, despite a winter splint problem, to triumph in that memorable 2,000 Guineas of 1989.

Hern had answered all the questions which the Palace decision had posed. With supreme irony it was Nashwan, the son of Height of Fashion, the mare the royal advisors had discarded in 1982, who proved the trainer was still right at the top of the tree. The scenes at Newmarket after Nashwan's victory were incredible. The endless applause as Carson rode Nashwan into the enclosure left no doubts whose side the racing world was on. Nashwan's subsequent successes throughout the 1989 season did nothing but ram home Hern's point. The Palace showed a degree of transigence when at the big York meeting in May, the scenes of emotion of Guineas day presumably digested, they announced that Hern would be able to share the West Ilsley facilities with William Hastings-Bass for the 1990 season, giving him more valuable time to find new premises. Finally, it was announced later in the summer that Hamdan al Maktoum, ever grateful for Hern's immaculate training of Nashwan, would find and build new stables to enable the trainer to continue his career. At the end of 1990 Hern's string left Hodcott. It was the end of an era.

Lord Carnarvon, the Queen's racing manager, was much criticized throughout the long saga. As a royal appointee, he was of course unable to put his case across publicly. Whose decision it was to terminate Hern's time at West Ilsley is a matter of conjecture, as neither of the sides has ever discussed the decision publicly. An interesting story, which did the rounds at the time, suggests that Carnarvon, contrary to popular belief, was not to blame at all.

A former racing personality, who later became distinguished in another walk of life, was asked to luncheon at the Palace in the company of others who had performed with distinction in their chosen field. The luncheon took place before Hern's 1988 illness. At the time, the trainer appeared to be a permanent fixture at his West Ilsley base. Seated next to the monarch, the guest, as both had a common interest, turned the talk to racing. As the conversation continued, the guest was surprised by some remarks his host made about her string of horses and the way they were campaigned. The luncheon ended, the guest took his leave. He did not think of the conversation until much later, when he read the announcement that Hern's lease would not be renewed. Recalling the tone of his talk many months before, he absorbed the news without a flicker of surprise. To this day he maintains Lord Carnarvon blameless and believes the decision was made in its entirety by the highest authority of all.

Since Hern's departure the royal string at West Ilsley has been short on class. William Huntingdon won the Ascot Gold Cup of 1991 with Indian Queen. However, she was the property of a longstanding patron of his stable Sir Gordon Brunton, not of the Queen. Huntingdon was groomed as Hern's successor many moons ago. He first received the royal horses in 1977 when he trained at Newmarket, and his succession to the post of main royal trainer always seemed assured. The timing was the surprising factor. The Queen is most knowledgeable on racing and breeding matters, taking her role as owner of Hodcott very seriously indeed. As often as her busy schedule permits, she visits the famous downs to watch her string in action. West Ilsley's proximity to Windsor and London was a principal reason why the royal horses arrived at Hodcott in the sixties and her patronage of Newmarket, the chosen training place of the majority of her royal predecessors, waned.

The Queen Mother's connection with the training grounds at Lambourn began later. In 1973 her friend and trainer, Peter Cazalet, died. Cazalet, who trained at Fairlawne in Kent, had handled the Queen Mother's jumpers for many years. The famous collapse of Devon Loch on the Aintree run-in had deprived Cazalet of certain National victory for his royal patron in 1956. On the dispersal of his stables, the Queen Mother's string moved to Fulke Walwyn at Upper Lambourn. On 23 November 1973 Walwyn saddled Game Spirit to win at Newbury, ridden by Aly Branford, to provide the Queen Mother with her first win from Saxon House. Many more successes were to follow until the last winner Walwyn would saddle for her. In the last few days of his last season's training in 1990, Gerald Oxley steered one of the Queen Mother's old favourites, The Argonaut, to victory at the tiny Norfolk course of Fakenham.

Game Spirit was a good class steeplechaser. Newbury was his favourite racecourse and his many triumphs there prompted the executive to name a race after him. Bill Smith rode many winners on Game Spirit, and it was he who partnered Tammuz to win the Schweppes of 1975 at Newbury in the royal colours. Tammuz, who was a son of Highclere's mother Highlight, was a full brother to the 1974 1,000 Guineas winner, being also by Queen's Hussar. After a flat career curtailed by leg problems, Tammuz was a gift from the Queen to her mother. In typical Walwyn fashion, he was produced fit on the right day with the right weight to record a notable royal triumph in one of the most difficult handicaps to win.

Special Cargo was another marvellous advertisement for Walwyn's training skill. For three years in a row he brought the almost crippled Special Cargo to his peak to win the Grand Military under Gerald Oxley in 1984, 1985 and 1986. The race particularly dear to the Queen Mother's heart is the feature of the famous military meeting at Sandown. After his 1984 triumph, Walwyn won the valuable sponsored handicap, the Whitbread Gold Cup, with Special Cargo. Looking unlikely to gain even a place jumping the last, the gallant Special Cargo responded to Kevin Mooney's every call to get up close home in one of the race's most exciting finishes. At the Queen Mother's ninetieth birthday celebrations Special Cargo and The Argonaut, resplendent in the royal colours, paraded past their proud owner, to remind the huge crowds watching of her long connection with the sport.

Still one of steeplechasing's greatest supporters in her nineties, the Queen Mother has continued to patronize the Saxon House yard of Cath Walwyn.

This year the Queen Mother for the first time became a patron of two other Lambourn yards. Jim Joel left her the choice of one of his jumpers in his will. She chose the 1992 Cheltenham Festival winner, Keep Talking. The promising horse will remain with his previous trainer, the former amateur rider, Tim Thomson Jones, who was Jim Joel's great nephew. His yard, The Croft in Upper Lambourn, is only a stone's throw from the Walwyn establishment at Saxon House. Nick Henderson will also train for the Queen Mother for the first time. Among the three horses he will have is the New Zealand-bred import Nearco Bay, the winner of New Zealand's Grand National.

A great judge of jumping form, the Queen Mother is reputed to like a bet occasionally. Managers of betting shops near her London home have learnt to recognize the various palace messengers. Experience has taught them that the information is generally good: the royal investment is therefore laid off accordingly!

Prince Charles has also patronized an Upper Lambourn stable. He chose Nick Gaselee, a former top-class amateur rider, to instruct him in the art of race-riding and find him a suitable mount. Their first choice, Allibar, finished second in a well contested amateur riders' handicap chase at Ludlow in October 1981.

Nick Gaselee fervently believes the Prince of Wales was not given the credit he deserved for this effort. He points out that the Prince had only ever ridden in one steeplechase before this effort, when he finished

Prince Charles leading his own horse, Allibar, back from morning exercise

fourth at Sandown on Sea Swell in a Hunter Chase. On his only previous ride he had finished second in a Plumpton flat race. The winner,
unbelievably, was the good chaser of the future, Classified. More unbelievably still, the winner was ridden by the current Channel Four presenter,
Derek Thompson.

Prince Charles's first ever ride in public at Plumpton on Long Wharf. He finished second to Classified ridden by the Channel Four racing presenter, Derek Thompson. The Prince is on the left of the photograph, Thompson and Classified on the right

Tragedy was to strike soon after: Allibar was to drop dead at exercise. A new horse was purchased quickly. The ex John Edwards-trained Good Prospect was, Gaselee believes with hindsight, the wrong type of horse to buy for an inexperienced rider. The horse had no front on him and consequently was hard to sit on if he made a mistake. In the Kim Muir at Cheltenham, Good Prospect made an error and unseated the Prince. He only had one other ride over hurdles before retiring from the saddle.

A few years ago the Prince asked Gaselee to buy him a Spartan General mare. Gaselee purchased Spartan Legacy from John Thorne's Warwickshire stud. Her produce from a mating with the stallion Remezzo was a horse named Devil's Elbow. In the future he was to win a race, only to lose it on a technicality.

Since the sixties the royal family had cemented its link with the training grounds of Berkshire. It was 201 years after her ancestor William, Duke of Cumberland's death when the present Queen sent her first batch of horses to West Ilsley. The royal connection with the county's premier racecourse Ascot was far more longstanding. They have been associated with the course ever since Queen Anne took that famous ride across the heath in the first decade of the eighteenth century.

8
ASCOT RACECOURSE

Ascot is the only British racecourse which belongs to the Crown. It is Berkshire's oldest racecourse and is its most renowned. The four-day Royal Meeting, held in June, is one of the foremost social occasions of the year and was the only racing that Ascot held until the Second World War. For many racegoers who attend the Royal Meeting, the social side of the event is of far greater importance than the excellent four days of racing which the meeting provides. Although Ascot is, as racecourses go, the jewel in Berkshire's crown, this was not always the case. A brief examination of the course's early history will prove the point.

After her famous ride Queen Anne decreed that a racecourse should be built on Ascot Heath. She placed the task in the capable hands of her friend and confidante the Duke of Somerset. History relates that the Duke accomplished his task cheaply, only spending £588 19s 5d. When the course was ready, the first meeting was held on 11 August 1711. On the second day of the meeting, a Monday, Queen Anne showed that she approved of her new invention. She sponsored a £100 race, named the Queen's Plate. Racing was a low key affair, with few meetings held. When Anne passed away in 1714, the meeting was cancelled in order that due mourning might be observed.

Queen Anne rewarded the Duke of Somerset by putting him in charge of racing at the course. His appointment created a precedent. For the next 190 years, the Master of the Buckhounds was responsible for Ascot whether he was interested in the sport or not. The buckhounds conducted their sport in the woods that surrounded the heath. Many rides were cut through Windsor Forest for the chase, and it was the result of a great chase, which culminated on the heath, that persuaded the Queen that it was the perfect venue for a racecourse. The open heath was well known by the Master as he hunted over it with regularity. There was method in the Queen's judgement when she chose Somerset to turn her dream into a reality.

History relates that the tradition of wearing morning dress at the Royal

Meetings originated as a result of the antics of a Miss Forester, an eccentric lady courtier of Queen Anne. At the first meeting she appeared dressed as a boy in britches, a long white riding coat and a small cocked hat. She is always credited with inventing the Ascot style of dress. It is more likely, however, that Queen Anne and her court were so appalled by Miss Forester's dress sense that from that day on it became an unwritten law, later a decree, that morning dress should be worn by those in the proximity of royalty when they were racing at Ascot.

When racing resumed in the next reign, it was a very local affair. Indeed, the 1720 August meeting was only open to horses that had hunted with the Royal Buckhounds. In 1730 a decent day of racing took place. The main event, a £50 plate, was won by the Duke of Newcastle's Fidler. Unfortunately the meeting was not a portent for the future of racing on the heath. After a three-day meeting in 1735 and 1736, and one in 1739, the course closed for the next five years. Unbelievably it had suffered from the effect of the Duke of Bolton's Act of Parliament, which was the cause of many meetings closing at the time. Ascot could not find the money to put on a £50 plate at each meeting, a condition of the act which applied to racing anywhere but Newmarket or Black Hambleton in Yorkshire. The hierarchy of racing did not attach much importance to Ascot as a venue for the sport.

William Duke of Cumberland, if not a friend to the clan MacDonald, was a great friend to Berkshire racing. From his stud not far away at Cranbourne Lodge, he set about restoring the fortunes of his local track at Ascot. As the Ranger of Windsor Forest he felt responsible for the course and took it under his wing. There is no doubt he saved it from an early demise. By his death in 1765 the course was firmly established, and it was then that the main meeting moved to June where it has always remained. In 1768 a five-day meeting was held, the same as in the present day.

In 1785 the Prince of Wales, later to be George IV, had his first winner at Ascot. In 1791 he won the Oatlands Stakes, a 2-mile sweepstake worth more than £3,000 to the winner (the Derby of 1791 was worth only £1,079) with Baronet ridden by Samuel Chifney. The Prince's other runner Escape, deserted by Chifney, finished down the field. Four thousand people reputedly watched racing on the heath that day. The Oatlands Stakes was moved in 1792 to Newmarket, and ceased to be a major race by the end of George IV's reign.

In 1793 the Prince lost his enthusiasm for racing as a result of a scandal concerning the same Escape, who ran in the 1791 Oatlands. In the October of 1791, Escape's performance in a race at Newmarket saw the stewards find that the Prince's horse had not been ridden to the best of his ability, and they severely reprimanded the royal jockey Chifney. The stewards based their findings on the fact that Escape had finished last in a race on one day and first the next day, beating Skylark who had finished miles ahead of him on the first occasion. Although the Prince's integrity was not questioned, Sir Charles Bunbury said that the Prince must sack Chifney or appear to be implicated. With commendable loyalty to his jockey the Prince refused and, sickened by the scandal, sold his string and did not return to the ranks of ownership for nine more years.

In 1825 the Prince, now George IV, instituted the Royal Procession, one of Royal Ascot's oldest traditions. Before racing begins, the royal family and their guests drive down the racecourse straight in five open landaus, accompanied by outriders, resplendent in scarlet jackets and gold braided top hats. This feature of the four days of the Royal Meeting has not changed since George IV instituted it over 160 years ago. In 1822 the distinguished architect Nash accepted a commission to build a royal pavilion for the Royal Family and their Windsor guests. An enclosure was tacked on to the front to enable all to watch the sport. This is the origin of the Royal Enclosure at the June meeting. All gentlemen must wear morning dress to gain admittance, even today.

In 1829 one of the great races for the Ascot Gold Cup was run. The field included two Derby winners, one St Leger winner, an Oaks winner and the previous year's Gold Cup winner. The race was won by Zinganee, bought by Lord Chesterfield on the eve of the great race for the then enormous sum of £2,500. Sam Chifney junior, son of Sam Chifney who had ridden George IV's Baronet in the Oatlands way back in 1791, rode the winner. The next year George IV was dead and William IV, the sailor king, was on the throne.

Ascot declined in popularity throughout the 1830s. William, although not enamoured by the turf, believed the royal family should patronize it. He believed the fact that the Gold Cup should only be open to horses owned by members of the Jockey Club, White's or Brook's was wrong. In 1831 the Gold Cup had only attracted two runners, and the King thought this a major factor in the course's increasing unpopularity. In 1836 affairs had reached an all-time low. Consequently the King gave a

The paddock at Ascot in Victorian times

dinner to discuss the decreasing standing of Ascot, the course which he owned.

To this dinner he invited various luminaries of the turf, including five dukes, eight earls, Lord George Bentinck, Charles Greville and a Colonel Peel. After much discussion, it was agreed that a new grandstand should be erected, and during race-weeks the Master of the Buckhounds should be helped by a member of the Jockey Club. The Earl of Essex was appointed to the task of supervising the building of the stand and in 1839 the first foundation stones were laid. A Grandstand Company was formed to finance the building, with a capital value of £10,000 at £100 a share. When the project was completed, the stand incorporated a weighing room, a jockeys' dressing room and a judge's office. The stand was the most modern of its time.

In 1838 Queen Victoria drove up the course, attended by Lord Melbourne. At dinner that evening she informed the politician that 'she had not betted as it bored her'. She was to attend the meeting until Prince Albert's death, but after that never went to Ascot again. However, her son the Prince of Wales was a regular visitor to Ascot. As a young man he wrote to his mother concerning the advantages of royal patronage of Ascot: 'It is an opportunity for the Royal Family to show themselves in public – which I am sure you desire – and after all racing with all its faults still remains, I may say, a National Institution of the country.' The Prince had significant successes at the meeting. In 1894 he won the St James's Palace Stakes with Florizel, the first good horse that his mare Perdita bred. She was later to be the dam of the Prince's Derby winners, Persimmon and Diamond Jubilee. All three of these excellent royal colts were by the legendary stallion, St Simon.

When Queen Victoria died in 1901, the Royal Meeting observed the traditions of mourning. The race cards were edged in black and on the first two days of the meeting visitors to the Royal Enclosure all wore black in memory of the Queen. In 1909 King Edward won the St James's Palace with his previous year's Derby winner Minoru. The next day the royal colours were first past the post again, the filly Princess de Galles winning the Coronation Stakes. Edward never visited another Royal Meeting. By the next one, he was dead. For the duration of the First

The Ascot Grandstand at the turn of the century

Pat Eddery and the 1975 Derby winner Grundy at Peter Walwyn's Seven Barrows yard

The Earl of Carnarvon, the Queen's racing manager and chairman of Newbury Racecourse, with his 1992 Royal Ascot winner, Niche

The Queen's Colour Sergeant winning the 1992 Royal Hunt Cup at Royal Ascot

The 1992 Royal Procession at Royal Ascot

Khaled Abdullah leading in his 1990 Derby winner Quest for Fame (Pat Eddery aboard). The trainer Roger Charlton is on the right

World War there was no racing at Ascot; the course being used as a military depot with the stand in the Silver Ring doubling as a hospital. In 1923 a royal victory was celebrated when Weathervane, ridden by Staff Ingham, later to train with distinction at Epsom, won the Royal Hunt Cup for George V. The King also won the Hardwicke Stakes with Limelight in 1933.

King George VI experienced some good times at the Royal Meeting. In 1941 he won the Coventry and the Queen Mary with Big Game and Sun Chariot respectively. Both carried the royal colours to success in Classic races the following year. In 1949 he won the Coronation Stakes with Avila ridden by Michael Beary. The present Queen has also won her fair share of prizes since her accession. Although Aureole's King George win in 1954 is the most notable, she won the 1959 St James's Palace with Above Suspicion and the 1957 Ribblesdale with Almeria. She emulated her grandfather George V by taking the 1953 Hunt Cup with Choir Boy, and her father George VI when she won the 1961 Coronation with Aiming High. For two successive years she took the King Edward VII Stakes in the late fifties with Restoration and Pindari. Hopeful Venture won the Hardwicke in 1968, and in 1979 the Queen's Expansive won the Ribblesdale and Buttress won the Queen's Vase. There was to be a long gap of thirteen years, though, before hats were raised to acknowledge another royal victory. In 1992 Colour Sergeant, without a previous run that season, took the Royal Hunt Cup for the Queen's principal trainer Lord Huntingdon.

In the Ascot paddock before Aureole won the 1954 Hardwicke, the Queen, anxious to hear if her favourite horse had a chance, asked his jockey, Eph Smith, if he thought that he would win. With great modesty, Smith replied: 'Well, Ma'am, we are rather handicapped. The horse is blind in one eye and I am deaf.'

One of the last Masters of the Buckhounds, the Lord Ribblesdale of the day, thought that the course should be relaid as the spectators' view was poor. He set up plans for the venture but it was not for another fifty years that anything was done. In 1946 King George VI approved plans for a massive reconstruction of the course. At the same time he suggested the course should hold three extra meetings, which would be known as Ascot Heath meetings. The course was improved in three ways. Firstly, the hill on the rise on the round course was cut back. Secondly, a dip on the Swinley course was filled with soil and the Swinley Bottom turn was remade to produce a more gentle corner where the course joins the Old Mile. Thirdly, the final turn into the straight was altered as the Royal Hunt Cup straight course was relaid. The result of these improvements moved the straight mile course further from the stands and virtually doubled the size of the enclosures. New lodges were built at the entrance to the new straight course, and a watering system was installed, served by sprinklers – the water coming from the reservoir which stands in the centre of the heath.

In 1947 the new turf was laid. It was given seven years to mature and was not raced on until 1955. This is the same course that is used now. The round course is right-handed, some 14 furlongs long; the straight course of one mile is a stiff test climbing uphill for the majority of its length. For some years afterwards the new course's drainage was inadequate and much work was done after the last two days of the 1964 Royal Meeting were abandoned, due to torrential rain. In the early sixties a steeplechase course was laid on the inside of the flat course. The turf was brought by lorries from the defunct racecourse at Hurst Park. In April 1965 the new jumping course was used for the first time. The first running of the famous sponsored handicap, the SGB Chase, was won by Arkle in 1966.

The improvements to the racetrack were followed by massive improvements to the stands. In 1961 the Queen Elizabeth stand was built by Wimpeys at a cost of £1m. On the top three tiers of the stand are 200 private boxes, which command an impressive view of the sport far below. The stand is incorporated within the Tattersalls enclosure. Three years later the Royal Enclosure stand was finished, the centrepiece being the royal box. Outside the weighing room stand two lions donated by Bernard, Duke of Norfolk, who served both King George VI and the present Queen in the capacity of His and then Her Majesty's Ascot Representative from 1945 to 1972. The post of the monarch's representative at Ascot dates back to the time of Edward VII. The Royal Buckhounds having been abolished, an act of Parliament, known as the Ascot Authority Act, was passed. The act empowered the sovereign to appoint a representative of the trustees of Ascot 'to promote the success, welfare and prosperity of Ascot races'. It added that the appointee should be subject only to the wishes of the sovereign. This was the origin of the position: the holder of the office being directly responsible to the reigning monarch, whose Crown Estates are the proprietors of the racecourse at Ascot.

Although much renovation, such as the new Queen Anne building, has been undertaken in recent years, the major stand and course improvements occurred in the Duke's term of office. As well as improving the facilities for both horse and spectator, he worked hard at improving the quality of racing at all the Ascot fixtures. With the then clerk of the course, Sir John Crocker-Bulteel, they founded the King George VI and Queen Elizabeth Stakes. Originally the Festival of Britain Stakes, it was first run in 1951 at the Ascot July meeting. It is now recognized as one of the world's most important races, in which the Classic horses of their generation take on their elders for the first time. Grundy's great duel with the four-year old Bustino in the seventies is many people's idea of the finest ever horse race. The present representative Sir Piers Bengough and the clerk of the course Nicky Beaumont have continued the Duke's policy, upgrading the facilities and racing at every available opportunity.

Recently the idea of a Festival of Racing was originated. The event, with the Group I Queen Elizabeth II Stakes as its highlight, is held at the September meeting. Sponsored originally by the beleaguered conglomerate Brent Walker, it is at present searching for an overall sponsor to maintain its position as one of the most valuable day's racing in the season. Ascot has been fortunate in its sponsors. De Beers, the South African diamond corporation, has been behind the July meeting for many years and SGB has been a permanent feature on the jumping card since 1965. Although sponsorship is a major priority for the executive, the races at the June four-day Royal Meeting are never sponsored. Traditionally the sport starts with the Queen Anne Stakes the first race on the Tuesday and ends with the marathon $2\,^3/_4$ mile Queen Alexandra the last race on the Friday. The order of the twenty-four races at the Royal Meeting is rarely altered. The St James's Palace Stakes was traditionally the last race on the Tuesday. In the early eighties it was moved to the middle of Tuesday's card, the authorities correctly surmising that it was a mistake to have the best race on the card run last. The splendid duel between the fine three-year-old milers Kris and Young Generation in the 1979 race did much to force the change.

Many of the races at the Royal Meeting have long histories. The Bessborough, the Coventry, the Hardwicke and the Ribblesdale are named after former Masters of the Royal Buckhounds. The New Stakes was renamed the Norfolk in honour of the 16th Duke's contribution to Ascot. This is the most recent change to a race name, although throughout

the ages other events, personages or buildings have been thus commemo-
rated. Examples are the Queen Mary, first run in 1921; named after
George V's queen, the Edward VII Stakes in 1926; the King's Stand in
1901; and the St James's Palace first run as long ago as 1834. The Royal
Hunt Cup, the big mile handicap run on the Wednesday of the meeting,
dates back to 1843. The meeting's showpiece, the Ascot Gold Cup run
on the Thursday, traditionally Ladies Day, was instituted in 1807, when
Queen Charlotte was present. Run over $2^1/_2$ miles, it is the meeting's
feature race. In modern times there have been calls for a reduction in its
distance. Its critics say it is now anachronistic, claiming horses nowadays
are not bred to race so far. At the moment the traditionalists are winning
the day. Ascot's greatest test appears safe for the present time.

In its long history the Gold Cup has seen some fine contests. Bizarre
was a good stayer, winning the race for two successive years in 1824 and
1825. In 1844 the Russian Emperor, Nicholas I, visited Ascot while staying as a guest of Queen Victoria at Windsor Castle. So much did he
enjoy the racing that he insisted on providing annually a plate of £500 in
value to be raced for in lieu of the Gold Cup. Diplomacy insisted that his
offer was accepted, and in recognition of his generous act, the Gold Cup
was renamed the Emperor's Plate. Luckily the race had reverted back to
its old title by the time of the Crimean war!

In 1850 the previous year's Derby and St Leger winner, The Flying
Dutchman, came down from Middleham in Yorkshire to win the Gold
Cup by an easy eight lengths. The 1865 Triple Crown winner Gladiateur, a French-bred colt, known universally as the 'Avenger of
Waterloo' because of the ease with which he disposed of his English-bred
opponents, won the Cup in 1866. His jockey Harry Grimshaw was so
shortsighted that he allowed Gladiateur to lie 300 yards behind the leader
at the Swinley Bottom turn. The French horse, realizing the problem,
picked up his bit and caught the other runners with such rapidity that he
was forty lengths clear at the finishing post. Gladiateur suffered from a
recurring lameness throughout his racing career. He must have been one
of the bravest as well as one of the best of Ascot Gold Cup winners.

Although Gladiateur was trained in England at Newmarket by Tom
Jennings, in 1874 a French-trained horse won. Boiard, the French Derby
winner of 1873, beat a tremendous field. Doncaster, the Epsom Derby
winner of 1873, Gang Forward, the 2,000 Guineas winner and Marie
Stuart, a previous Oaks and Leger winner were among the vanquished

English. In 1884 St Simon, never entered for a Classic race, produced a memorable Gold Cup performance. He trounced the previous year's Gold Cup victor Tristam by twenty lengths. Tristam proved the value of St Simon's performance by winning the Hardwicke on the following day. St Simon subsequently became one of the turf's greatest sires, being champion sire for seven seasons in a row.

One of the gamest mares to win the Gold Cup was Lord Stanley's Oaks winner, Quashed. In 1936 she beat the great American-bred stayer Omaha by a short head after a tremendous battle the whole way up the finishing straight. Great cheers resounded as the gallant mare returned to the unsaddling enclosure. Her brave effort, however, took so much out of her that she never won again and proved a total failure when she went to stud. In 1949 Lord Derby's Alycidon avenged his St Leger defeat by Black Tarquin. In a great struggle from the bend, Alycidon finally gained the upper hand to score by five lengths. Alycidon was a marvellous stallion, Alcide being his best colt. Nowadays owners are loath to campaign their Classic horses over the extreme distance of the cup races, feeling it devalues them as stallions. Blakeney, as long ago as 1970, was the last Derby winner to contest a Gold Cup. In the last century it was the rule rather than the exception.

For this reason the race has arguably in recent times lost much of its class. Some great stayers, on the other hand, have won it since the war. Fighting Charlie trained by Freddie Maxwell was the first horse to win the Gold Cup twice since the war. Rock Roi won it twice, only to be disqualified on both occasions in the early seventies. In 1975 the fine French stayer Sagaro won for the first time: victories in 1976 and 1977 proved him to be the Ascot specialist of modern times. Ridden in all his Ascot wins by Lester Piggott, his impressive blend of stamina and acceleration did much to increase the standing of the race and its profile in the public eye. In recent years Le Moss and Ardross both won successive Gold Cups for Henry Cecil's Newmarket stable. In 1984 and 1985 Barry Hills replied for Lambourn with Gildoran winning on both occasions. In 1991 the mare Indian Queen took the famous race, emulating another representative of the fairer sex, the brave Quashed.

In the old days, the potential Classic colts and fillies regularly plundered the Royal Ascot two-year-old prizes. Sun Chariot and Big Game's 1941 victories in the Queen Mary and the Coventry are good examples. For a time they seemed to become the preserve of the earlier sprint-bred type. Then Mill Reef's win in the Coventry of 1970 seemed to prove that no harm befell a Classic horse running as early as the Royal Meeting. In recent years the Coventry, especially, has been contested by animals destined to reach the highest class in their three-year-old year. Sun Prince won the Coventry of 1972 and later turned into a miler of tremendous ability. More recently in 1983, Chief Singer won the race on his debut before going on to far better things. Sure Blade and Horage, also winners of the Coventry in the eighties, later went on to win the St James's Palace Stakes at three. The 1991 and 1992 Derby winners Generous and Dr Devious both finished second in the Coventry in their respective two-year-old years. The race has now regained its prestige and is recognized again as a stepping stone to the Classics of the following year.

The three-year-old group races still attract the proven Classic performers. The St James's Palace is usually the mid-season target for the 2,000 Guineas winner, if he is to be campaigned as a miler. The Coronation Stakes, the fillies' equivalent, can be similarly described. The races for the older horses have decreased in standing only in the respect that fewer three-year-olds are these days kept in training at four. The handicaps are most competitive affairs with many runners, and are great gambling mediums. The great weight-carrying performance of Irish Elegance in the twenties in the Royal Hunt Cup was rivalled when the Lester Piggott ridden Jumping Hill, with 9 st. 7 lb. on his back, pulverized his field in 1976. A year before, Piggott had been the perpetrator of another legendary weight-carrying performance when the fine Irish sprinter Boone's Cabin humped 10 st. to victory in the Wokingham.

Ascot's greatest equine favourite was the grand old stayer Brown Jack. The winner of the Champion Hurdle as a four-year-old, Brown Jack owed his subsequent flat success to the jockey Steve Donoghue. Having seen Brown Jack's Cheltenham win, Donoghue suggested to his trainer, Aubrey Hastings, that the horse should try his luck on the flat. Brown Jack raced fifty-five times on the flat and won eighteen races. He won the Queen Alexandra Stakes on the Friday of Royal Meeting for six years in a row in the thirties. His last Queen Alexandra victory was too much for his then trainer Ivor Anthony. He could not bear to watch the race, preferring to sit under a tree in the paddock. Only when he heard the rousing cheers from the stand did he realize that Brown Jack had won again. Although the Irish horse was best known for his Ascot triumphs and subsequently had a race named after him, he won an Ebor and a

Goodwood Cup to add to his Champion Hurdle. The sight of Brown Jack and Donoghue winning the meeting's final race was a standing dish in the years before the Second World War.

If Brown Jack was Ascot's most popular horse, Lester Piggott has been the most popular jockey. No less than eleven Gold Cups have fallen his way. Starting in 1957 with Zarathusa, his last victory was in 1982 on Ardross. His domination of the July feature, the King George VI and Queen Elizabeth, is almost as complete. He has won it seven times, firstly in 1965 on Meadow Court. His score is likely to be substantially larger when he chooses to retire for the second time.

Ascot, like all places with a history, has tragedy intermingled with its success. In 1913 an Old Harrovian, Harold Hewitt, a moralist who disapproved strongly of the turf, jumped in front of the Gold Cup field some 7 furlongs from home on the bottom bend. Pointing a loaded revolver at the fast approaching field, he was struck by the leading horse's head. Tracery, the previous year's Derby third, was brought down and his rider Snowy Whalley, later to train at Compton, was unseated, though he was not harmed. Prince Palatine, trained at Whatcombe in Berkshire, won the race for the second successive year.

In 1930 a flash of lightning caused a racegoer to be struck down dead. But the greatest tragedy of all was when the fine jockey Manny Mercer, brother of Joe, was killed on 26 September 1959, aged only twenty-nine. Mercer was unseated from Priddy Fair while cantering to the start. His head hit the concrete rail, and in addition the filly kicked him in the face. The last race of the day was abandoned as a mark of respect. Manny Mercer was married to Susan Wragg, daughter of the famous jockey and trainer, Harry Wragg. Their daughter Carolyn is now married to the champion jockey, Pat Eddery. At the time of his death Mercer had ridden 100 winners that season, a feat he had accomplished on four previous occasions. Manny Mercer was reputed to sew his money inside the cushions in his home. One day a wicked colleague sent him a telegram saying that his house was on fire: until he realized it was a hoax, Mercer was a worried man.

In 1973 one of the most promising jumping novices ever was killed as a result of an Ascot fall. The Fred Winter-trained Killiney was thought by many experts to be a surefire future Gold Cup winner. The Heinz Chase that day was to have been his last run of the season. A race is run at Ascot in his memory today.

If Ascot's June Royal Meeting attracts the leaders of the social sets, it also attracts the great gamblers. The market is traditionally the strongest of all at the Royal Meeting. Some great gambles have been landed, many have been lost. One of the most successful post-war punts was when Old Lucky won the 1974 Hunt Cup. Backed down to 8–1 to take a fortune from the ring, the trainer Bernard van Cutsem when asked by the press the winner's future plans, replied simply and succinctly: 'That was the plan.'

Although great horses and great races are a feature of Ascot's history, some owners like to run their horses for the prestige whether they are good enough or not. Some years ago an eccentric owner in James Bethell's Chilton stable made the trainer run a very moderate beast in the final event on the Friday, the Queen Alexandra Stakes. The animal was so outclassed that by the final mile it was nearly 2 furlongs behind the nearest horse. Bethell was appalled to see the cars from the car park in the centre of the track exiting before his runner reached the finishing straight. Forced to halt, until the attendant realized the race was not entirely done, the horse eventually finished the contest slower than any contestant had before.

Nowadays the popularity of the Royal Meeting is incredible. Huge crowds and traffic jams are features of the event. The Ascot Authority's London office has had so many new applications for entry to the Royal Enclosure in recent years that the majority are placed on a waiting list. The lucky ones are accepted in their first few years only on the Friday, traditionally the quietest day. If standards are not as rigid as they were in the past (for many years divorced persons were unable to obtain entry to the Royal Enclosure), the authorities are strict about behaviour and insist for the Royal Meeting that the correct form of dress is worn. Ladies in over-revealing dresses have been refused entry in the past, while raucous behaviour is also frowned on. The authorities did not react kindly when the wife of a distinguished bloodstock agent rode a gateman's bicycle round the unsaddling enclosure. Neither were they pleased when a famous film actress borrowed someone else's Royal Enclosure badge. She was summarily evicted regardless of her standing.

Ascot may seem to many outmoded. Its traditions and dress requirements seem to some to be a product of a bygone age. Those who scoff at the traditions never could deny that the Royal Meeting's racing is always first rate. Rarely do so many top horses compete over four days in a single place. After all, Queen Anne originally designed the course for racing horses. In that respect Ascot has few peers, and the standard of sport has not diminished over the years. If in some ways Ascot still lives in the past, those responsible for its development since the war could not in general be accused of intransigence or failure to move with the times. The foundation of the jumping course and the increase in flat fixtures are proof enough of that. Unlike some of the country's other courses it has tried when possible to adapt to the needs of the modern age and the modern racegoer.

9

THE RACECOURSES OF NEWBURY AND WINDSOR

Newbury

The racecourse at Newbury, which lies on the south-east side of the town in between Greenham Common and the railway line, owed its foundation to the vision of the great Victorian trainer of seven Derby winners, John Porter of Kingsclere. Although racing had taken place in the proximity of Newbury in the past, the meetings on Wash Common and Enborne Heath being examples, by the end of the nineteenth century Newbury had no racecourse to its name.

John Porter had for many years, when travelling from Newbury to London by rail, viewed the ground between Greenham Common and the railway, from the window of his carriage. The more he saw of it, the more he thought it would make a perfect racecourse. It was virtually flat, near to the town and railway and more importantly it was close to the training grounds of Berkshire, Hampshire and Wiltshire. He was sure the local trainers would patronize such a place in large numbers. He sought out the owner of the land, L.H. Baxendale. Mr Baxendale thought Porter's idea a good one. The two men formed a syndicate and drew up plans. When the plans were ready, Porter approached the Jockey Club to gain their approval.

Porter's original quest to build the racecourse was fraught with difficulty: his detailed plans were thrown out by the Jockey Club. Legend has it that he met King Edward VII, whom he had trained for in the past, one day in Newmarket High Street as he was leaving the Jockey Club meeting, where his plans for the new racecourse had been rejected yet again. His meeting with the sovereign was fortuitous. On hearing of Porter's problem, the King asked if he could examine the plans. Summoning Porter to see him the very next day, he informed the trainer that he believed, if a fresh application was submitted, the Jockey Club would view it in a more favourable light. The King was correct in his assumption. At his

John Porter, the great Kingsclere trainer, and founder of Newbury racecourse

next meeting Porter was granted his licence. Newbury racecourse was born.

On 26 September 1905, the course was ready. The first meeting was attended by 15,000 people. The racecard made impressive reading. The Dukes of Portland and Westminster, Viscount Falmouth, Lord Howard de Walden, Sir R.W. Jardine, William Bass, forebear of the Queen's present trainer Lord Huntingdon, L.W. Baxendale, James Buchanan, John Musker, Washington Singer and Philip Wroughton, the owner of the famous Whatcombe gallops, were all listed as patrons of the new venture. The stewards at that first meeting were the Earls of Coventry, Durham, Carnarvon and Crewe, Lord Arthur Grosvenor and Mr W. Rayner. With such distinguished figures lending their support and with Porter himself listed as managing director, the venture could hardly fail.

The first race, the Whatcombe Handicap over 5 furlongs was won by Copper King. Atty Persse won the nursery seller with Theodore and had four more winners over the two-day inaugural meeting. Lord Carnarvon won three races on the first day including the Inaugural Handicap with Missovaya, trained at Whatcombe by Dick Dawson, later to be the trainer of three Derby winners. The most apt success occurred in the last race on the second day when John Porter, the course's founder, saddled Zealous to take the prize back to his famous Kingsclere yard.

Under Porter's guidance the course thrived. Retiring from training at the end of that season, he concentrated all his efforts on developing his brainchild, continuing as the racecourse company's managing director until his death in 1922. Many of the famous races run in the present day were established in those early years. The Newbury Spring Cup was first

The first race at Newbury's inaugural meeting in 1905. Copper King is the winner

run in 1906 and the same year the Greenham Stakes, which quickly became recognized as a 2,000 Guineas trial, was started. In 1909 King Edward VII's Minoru won the Greenham ridden by Herbert Jones. Later that year he was to carry the royal colours to Classic success in the 2,000 and the Derby. In 1909 the first Autumn Cup was run. The race, at that time a staying event run over 2 miles 1 furlong, was won by The White Knight, ridden by the fine American jockey 'Skeets' Martin. The White Knight was later to become one of the most formidable stayers of the age, winning the Ascot Gold Cup on two occasions. The Summer Cup was also to figure as an Ascot Gold Cup trial. In the twenties Tangiers and Santob both won it before going to score at Ascot. The steeplechase course was first used in 1906, and like its flat counterpart rapidly became popular and well patronized.

Established as one of the major courses, Newbury raced on a reduced scale in the first years of the First World War. However, racing was finally stopped in 1916, and the course then assumed a variety of positions. First it became a prisoner of war camp, then a munitions inspection depot, a hay dispersal depot, and finally a tank testing and repair site. The buildings and track survived their wartime use though, and in 1919 Newbury resumed racing. Twenty-four of the country's other courses were tragically to close in those difficult years between the wars. Newbury was an exception, and it continued to consolidate its position as one of the leading racecourses until the Second World War.

Newbury was not so lucky during the Second World War. Although racing took place until 1941, the course was then requisitioned for military use. In 1942 the United States Armed Forces took up residence there, and Newbury became the Americans' main British supply depot. John Porter must have turned in his grave when he saw the fate of his beloved course. The famous turf was covered in concrete and numerous railway tracks. The stables housed prisoners of war rather than equine champions. The Members' Bar became the American Officers' Mess. When the fixture list was published in 1946, Newbury's name was not on it.

Luckily for the course, the famous racing administrator Geoffrey Freer devoted his energies to restoring racing at the Berkshire course. Before he could start, Freer had to wait until the Marshall Plan was implemented in 1947. The Marshall Plan returned requisitioned land to its previous owners and found new places to store the enormous amounts of military equipment which had accumulated throughout the country during the

Newbury racecourse – a scene of devastation after the American forces had vacated the site at the end of the Second World War

war years. In June 1947 the course was released, and Freer put his rescue plan into operation. His task at first was thought by some to be impossible. The huge quantities of cement and rail track were slowly and carefully moved. The straight 5 furlong was relaid with turves provided from a nursery, which had been laid down with commendable perspicacity in 1944. The nursery had only enough turf for this five furlong stretch. The rest of the turf was obtained from a nearby housing development. Incredibly Freer's efforts finally against all the odds came to fruition. In 1949, on All Fools' Day, Newbury held its first post-war meeting.

Those who had visited the course's last fixture in 1941 were greeted with a redesigned circuit. The dog-leg in the back straight, which had been a feature of Porter's original design, was removed. The bends were made much gentler and Newbury became one of the fairest, most galloping courses in the land. Stan Mellor, the champion National Hunt jockey was moved in later years to describe Newbury as 'the best course in

England'. The course honoured Geoffrey Freer's notable contribution. As its undoubted saviour, he was rewarded by having a stand and a race named in his honour. The Geoffrey Freer Stakes is a pattern race run at Newbury in the summer, and the stand in the Silver Ring is known as the Geoffrey Freer Stand and was built in 1966.

Further improvements have been made since Freer's day. The Newbury management built a new stand in the members' enclosure in the seventies. It is possible for racegoers to view the sport from behind glass windows in the upper reaches of the stand. At the time this was seen as a great innovation, bringing racegoers to the course whatever the weather. At present a huge new development of the old members' stand opposite the winning post and the Tattersalls stand next door is being undertaken.

Some eighty years old and constructed of wood, the former stand would not have passed the new Safety of Sports Grounds Act. The new stand under construction, named the New Berkshire Stand, boasts impressive weighing room facilities facing the paddock. It has a large concourse on the ground floor. Escalators rise to the first floor where extensive eating and watching facilities are available. The members' and Tattersalls portions are to have many seats to enable the racegoer to watch the sport in comfort. The racecourse executive believes that over 10,000 more square feet is now available to the racegoers in these enclosures than was the case in the past. Above the viewing tier are thirty boxes, and above these on the very top is a modern press room with fantastic views of the racecourse. The new stand is designed to cater for functions other than racing; a most necessary aspect in the modern racecourse's life. Nowadays a course must utilize its assets for as many days as possible. Gone are the days when they were used exclusively on the relatively few days they raced. Much of the design has been based on the new track at Arlington Park, Chicago, which was rebuilt after being destroyed by fire. Arlington is seen as the ultimate in modern racecourse design. If work finishes on schedule, the new development will celebrate its opening with the 1992 Hennessy fixture.

A former Jockey Club handicapper, like his predecessor Geoffrey Freer, the soon to retire Clerk of the Course Charles Toller has been responsible for many improvements and innovations. The Compton Chase, a recognized Grand National trial, was his invention. With the support of the Osgood family (three successive generations have been course managers at Newbury) he has created a racing surface renowned countrywide. Local trainers often seek permission to gallop their horses on the springy turf of the back straight. Paul Cole put the finishing touches on Generous's Derby preparation with a Newbury racecourse gallop. Improved drainage has helped to eliminate the need for a high draw in sprint races. Years ago a horse was thought to have no chance if drawn on the far side. The good sprinter Record Token, later to win a Vernon's Sprint, was allowed by the bookmakers to start at a ridiculous price in the seventies in a two-year-old event. They thought he could not possibly win from his number one draw. His subsequent victory was viewed with amazement, his class eliminating any disadvantage. Charles Toller also reintroduced a selling race at the summer charity meeting which has proved to be a good source of income, as the charity take what is usually a substantial surplus. A recent innovative idea of the present racecourse chairman, Lord Carnarvon, is the Newbury Sales Super sprint, a very valuable event for two-year-olds bought at auction at the various sales. Designed for horses purchased below a figure of 30,000 gns, it gives the smaller stables a chance of taking a good prize as many of the expensive Arab-owned two-year-olds are disqualified from running. Aptly, Lord Carnarvon won the first running of the race in 1992, with his flying filly Lyric Fantasy, previously the winner of Ascot's Queen Mary. In recent years Newbury has started evening meetings again, with the emphasis on a family day out.

The famous Guineas trials, the Greenham and Fred Darling Stakes, are run at the April meeting. Rodrigo de Triano, subsequently to win two Guineas, was beaten on his seasonal debut in the Greenham. Often the ground is soft for these trials and shocks are somewhat commonplace. The subsequent Derby winner Grundy was beaten in the Greenham of 1975 by the fitter but vastly inferior colt, Mark Anthony. The dual Classic heroine of 1990, Salsabil, started her season with a comfortable Fred Darling victory. Another feature of the spring meeting is the John Porter Stakes, a mile-and-a-half race for four-year-olds and upwards. Distinguished past victors are the subsequent Arc winner Rheingold and the unlucky loser of two Ascot Gold Cups, Rock Roi.

The feature of the May meeting is the Lockinge Stakes. A dead heat occurred here in 1984 when Cormorant Wood, later that year to win a Benson and Hedges Gold Cup, and John Dunlop's Wassl were unable to be split by the judge. Started in 1958, the first two runnings of the race went to the Queen's colt, Pall Mall. His initial win as a three-year-old created a precedent. Three-year-olds are favoured by the weight conces-sion from the older generations, which they are entitled to in May: the Lockinge has proved a happy hunting ground for them. In 1978 the Ryan Price-trained Jellaby was clear with a furlong to run. Suddenly the huge grey horse lost his footing. He slipped and threw his rider Brian Taylor underneath the rail. He was the unluckiest loser ever of the Lockinge Stakes.

Two more pattern races, the Geoffrey Freer and the Hungerford are run at the August fixture. In September the 6-furlong Mill Reef Stakes for two-year-olds commemorates the fine Derby winner. Mill Reef was trained by Ian Balding at John Porter's old stables at Kingsclere, and won the Greenham on the way to his memorable Guineas defeat at the hands of Brigadier Gerard. The Newbury October Flat meeting features the 7-furlong Horris Hill Stakes for two-year-olds and the St Simon, a mile-and-a-half group race for three-year-olds and upwards.

As John Porter rightly forecast, Newbury is well patronized by local stables. It is also favoured by the major Newmarket yards. Henry Cecil has in recent years made a habit of plundering the maiden races at the Spring meeting with a string of good-class animals. The two-year-old events are frequently won by horses of high-class potential. Brigadier Gerard opened his account in the Berkshire Stakes at the June meeting, starting at the incredible price of 100–7 in a field of only five runners. The ill-fated Derby winner of 1981, Shergar, made his debut at New-bury's September meeting, impressing all with the ease of his success. Frank Morby, who rode in England in the seventies before emigrating to Kenya where he was leading jockey for many years, never rated the form of Newbury two-year-old races. Morby believed that it was possible to finish in the first six with a moderate beast, as many of the better contes-tants were invariably required to finish way out of the numbers. Their shrewd handlers did not want to attract the attention of the handicapper to animals of promise at this early stage in their careers.

Newbury's most popular race day is undoubtedly the Saturday in November when the Hennessy Gold Cup is run. Moved from Chelt-enham in 1960, it is steeplechasing's greatest early season test. One of the biggest shocks in the race's distinguished history was when Stalbridge Colonist defeated Arkle in the twilight of the great Irish horse's career. Many thought that Pat Taafe never realized that Stalbridge Colonist was a danger. Stan Mellor placed Stalbridge Colonist on Arkle's tail in the final stages. Pulling him out at the last, Mellor was gone before Taffe could take evasive action. Ken Cundell, the trainer of Stalbridge Colonist, later told Mrs Dreaper, the wife of Arkle's trainer Tom, that Arkle could not have been right. He believed his horse would never have beaten the Irish chaser in his heyday, even receiving the 31 lb. which Arkle gave the Cundell horse that day. Cundell was paying Arkle some form of compliment. Stalbridge Colonist was later to be narrowly beaten in two Gold Cups. The Lambourn trainer Fulke Walwyn loved the race, winning it many times in his career.

Newbury's other major jumping prize is the Schweppes Gold Trophy. Now known as the Tote Gold Trophy, it has been moved to the March meeting from its original February date because inclement weather caused several abandonments. The race assumed a degree of notoriety almost from its inception. Ryan Price lost his licence as a result of Rosyth's victory in the first Newbury running of the race in 1964. The stewards deemed the horse had not been allowed to run on his merits before the race. Later Price was to train Hill House to win the Newbury race, only to see him tested positively for steroids. Price, terrified he would lose his licence again, attempted to prove his innocence. Finally after many hearings and veterinary tests, Price was able to prove that the horse manufactured the steroids within his own system. Therefore they had not been injected or administered by an outside party. Whatever else, Schweppes gained far more publicity out of Hill House's victory than their advertising men could ever have imagined. In those early years the Epsom training family of Sutcliffe landed two formidable gambles in the race, John Sutcliffe junior winning with Elan and his father John senior with Cala Mesquida. One of the shortest priced favourites for the race was the Bob Turnell-trained Bird's Nest. Bird's Nest appeared thrown in at the weights, but backers lost their money when the horse fell at the second hurdle.

One day the actor Wilfrid Hyde-White was asked to stand in as a steward at Newbury. During an exciting finish, the senior steward was somewhat surprised to see the actor leaning markedly to his right. When the race was over, he turned to Hyde-White to ask him why he had assumed this strange posture during the final stages of the race. The senior steward was amazed when Hyde-White replied: 'You would have leant towards the winning post, my boy, if you had had 500 quid on the second!'

The great Manton trainer George Todd was once summoned in front of the Newbury stewards to explain the poor previous performances of a horse in his charge, which had just won. The senior steward, sure that Todd had been guilty of restraining his animal in earlier races to obtain a better price at Newbury, was determined to catch Todd out. Thinking he would prove Todd's guilt, he informed the trainer that the panel knew that Todd had had a very substantial bet. The panel were nonplussed when the trainer replied: 'Not so, I only had 500 on it.'

Newbury's constitution gives the racegoer a perfect view. The track is 1 mile and 7 furlongs long. The straight course is a mile in length. There is also a round-mile start, which is situated on a furlong spur, which joins the course proper at the 7-furlong start. The track is 80 yards wide on the bends and 90 in the straight. Its nature makes it one of the fairest tracks, as it is galloping: hard luck stories are therefore rare. The steeple-chase course is set inside the flat race circuit. Unlike many courses, the hurdlers do not race on the flat ground in the winter. The course is served by an efficient pop-up watering system, so complaints about hard going are very rare.

Newbury has one of the largest memberships of any of Britain's courses. The track has its own station just beyond the paddock, and many visitors travel from London on the race trains. Generally the class of racing is good. Newbury is a popular track to ride, and the professionals riding under both codes believe it to be one of the best racecourses: the new stand will make it one of the most modern. As one of Britain's youngest courses, it has accomplished much in its relatively short history. It is an apt memorial to the master trainer, John Porter of Kingsclere.

Windsor

In 1865 John Frail, of the distinguished family of turf administrators submitted plans for a racecourse on Clewer Meadows to the west of the town of Windsor. Later renamed Rays Meadow, it is the site of Windsor racecourse today. The River Thames runs along the northern boundary of the track, while the Mill Stream, which leaves the main river upstream of the course just above the 6-furlong start, rejoins the Thames down-river of the racecourse. Therefore the land on which the course stands is an island, surrounded by the Thames or the Mill Stream on every side.

Although racing had taken place in the Windsor Great Park in Henry VIII's time and Charles II and Queen Anne had been regular visitors to the course at Datchet Ferry a few miles down river, Windsor had had no permanent meeting of note since Datchet Ferry had fallen from grace when Queen Anne decided to concentrate her racing on the Ascot Heath. John Frail saw an opening for a course in the area to cater for the more moderate type of horse. Ascot nearby was the preserve of the better animal and only held one yearly fixture, the four-day Royal Meeting in June.

On 5 and 6 June 1866, Windsor held its first meeting at Rays Meadow. Present at the inaugural meeting were some famous turf figures. Admiral Rous, by then the Jockey Club's official handicapper as well as a Steward of the club, attended, as did the Marquess of Hastings, not long afterwards to be reduced to penury and early death, a victim of the dishonesty of his trainer, John Day of Danebury. In 1876 Fred Archer won the Surly Hall Welter Handicap over five furlongs on Aristocrat. The little course continued to thrive, happy to cater for the second-class horse, its picturesque riverside setting attracting good crowds up until the Great War.

Windsor was one of the seven courses permitted to race during the First World War. Although many factions not over-enamoured with the turf believed that racing should be stopped, Lloyd-George's government kept the sport going on a reduced scale, surmising that total closure would have a severely detrimental effect on the important bloodstock industry. In 1926, the year of the General Strike, the riverside course made the front pages of the newspapers. Winston Churchill, Stanley Baldwin's Chancellor of the Exchequer, had imposed a very unpopular betting tax. The bookmakers chose Windsor to make their protest, refusing to trade and going on strike. The action was to prove a success, as the government rapidly abolished the tax. Churchill, attending Windsor races in 1949 to see his Colonist II win the Lime Tree Stakes, was greeted with a far warmer reception from the bookmakers than he would have had in 1926. In 1923 Windsor was the scene of a rare occurrence, a triple dead heat in the Royal Borough Handicap at the September meeting. Even stranger was the fact that Gardner, the rider of Dumas, one of the three dead heaters, had been involved in another triple dead heat at Sandown eight years earlier. The Windsor dead heat is on pictorial record, captured by an on-the-ball photographer from the *Illustrated London News*.

Windsor was also permitted to stage racing during the Second World War. Salisbury and Newmarket were the only two other southern courses to do so. On 23 April 1943, great celebrations occurred when Gordon Richards won on Scotch Mist. Statisticians of the day believed this victory had enabled the jockey to pass Fred Archer's career total of 2,749 winners. Later research revealed that in fact Archer had only ridden 2,748 victorious mounts, and Windsor had to forego the credit for providing Sir Gordon with his notable achievement.

In 1944 a doodle bug cut out above the racecourse just as the jockeys were preparing to mount for the third race. In the ensuing panic, people rushed for cover. Gordon Richards, who was riding for the portly trainer Vernel Hobbs, ended up in the flower bed in the parade ring with the huge trainer on top of him. Until Ascot started to hold its Heath fixture on the Saturday after the Royal Meeting in the post-war years, Windsor held a very popular fixture where many of those who had lost at Ascot sought to get their money back before returning home. In the present day the course holds an evening fixture on the Monday before the Royal Meeting. The market here is often strong, as the big players seek to obtain some funds to bet with at the Royal Meeting.

In 1947 severe flooding of the Thames caused £10,000 worth of damage to the course. The water stood some 3 ft deep in the stands. John

Windsor Races: The Little Poem (D. Dineley) wins at a well-attended evening fixture in 1975

Knight, who had succeeded the Frails as manager, built a new weighing room and offices. There were not enough funds to rebuild the small stands, which still remain, mostly unaltered. In 1964 Windsor held the first of the Monday evening fixtures, which attract enormous crowds throughout the summer. When Alexandra Park, London's only race-course, closed in 1970, Londoners came in huge numbers to patronize Windsor's evening fixtures. The M4 motorway made the track even more accessible from London. Although facilities and the standard of the sport are moderate, the course makes no bones about the quality of its sport. The objective remains the same as in John Frail's day. The executive frames races of low value to attract large fields. It is hard to argue with this policy, as the course is always extremely well attended. In 1988 the course was purchased by Thompson Investments, and although some new boxes have been built, improvements to the stands are still awaited. The owners, seeing a healthy profit, presumably feel disinclined to plunge vast sums of money into a major rebuilding programme in these times of recession.

The racetrack is flat, set in the form of a figure of eight. In 1966 the second loop, which lies up-river from the stands, was redesigned. The original loop had been only 190 yards in radius and was very tight to negotiate. The new loop has a radius of 400 yards and rides much better. The nature of the course means that horses are racing on a bend for much of the longer races. Consequently the long striding galloping horse tends not to be suited to the twists and turns. The 5- and 6-furlong courses have an elbow over 2 furlongs from home. A high draw is a tremendous advantage in sprint races. Those jockeys favoured by the draw aim for a fast start to claim the standside rail: those drawn further out suffer a major disadvantage as they have to negotiate the elbow in the centre of the course, losing vital ground. Conversely, on soft ground the jockeys prefer to race on the opposite side of the course. A low draw is required in this eventuality. The longest flat race at Windsor is over 1 mile 3 furlongs 150 yards, and starts opposite the stands. The bend beyond the stands is deemed too sharp to turn at racing pace and therefore longer flat races are precluded.

Although the prize money is poor, the racing ground is generally well watered, the Thames being a superb natural reservoir. Trainers therefore are prepared to send a decent flat racer to Windsor as the track is very accessible for the training centres of Newmarket, Lambourn and Epsom as a result of the modern motorways. The fast two-year-old Formidable, the 1977 Middle Park winner, for instance, was beaten on his first ever outing at Windsor. Sea Music in 1971 won at Windsor on the Monday evening before Goodwood, before winning the Rous Memorial on the Sussex track only three days later. The three-year-old maiden events, often held as the evening's last race, can throw up a decent animal. The big Newmarket stables often prefer to win at a minor meeting, as the handicappers traditionally tend to treat victories at the less fashionable venues more leniently. The most valuable flat race at Windsor is the Winter Hill Stakes, a mile-and-a-quarter listed race, run at the last August meeting. The Winter Hill Stakes often attracts a top grade horse.

The steeplechase course at Windsor runs outside the flat course on the first loop, but moves inside for the second loop. The hurdles are run on the flat course, and the fences are not traditionally hard. Windsor's most valuable race, the New Year's Day Hurdle, is run at the New Year meeting. It often attracts Champion Hurdle candidates on their way to Cheltenham in March. The Fairlawne Chase run at the February meeting also attracts a good type of steeplecaser. Bula won the 1975 version of the race as part of his preparation for the Gold Cup, in which he finished third to Ten Up.

When the fine steeplechase jockey Philip Blacker retired from race riding to become a sculptor of renown, he was approached to act as a steward at Windsor. A day or so before his first official outing he banged his head against an errant cupboard door. As a result of this altercation, he attended Windsor with a black eye of formidable proportions. Although his colleagues eyed his injury with a few strange looks at the pre-race lunch, his first day went well until a trainer, for whom he had ridden in the past, was required to visit the stewards to explain the non-participation of one of his horses. The stipendary, as is the custom, introduced the panel to the trainer. As the stipendary mentioned Blacker's name, the trainer caught sight of his former rider's injured eye and, to Blacker's horror, exclaimed: 'Hello there, Phil. Been fighting again?'

When Windsor moved its stables to their present position, next to the racecourse, from the old location nearer the Maidenhead road, Willie Stephenson's travelling head lad, unaware the stables had been relocated, drove his horse box into the former stable yard one foggy morning. As the weather was cold and frosty and he could see no sign of life, he thought the meeting must have been abandoned. Turning his vehicle round without more ado, he headed hotfoot back to Royston. On his arrival home, he was greeted by a furious trainer, wanting to know why on earth his runners had not fulfilled their Windsor engagements.

Further drama occurred at the Thames-side course in the seventies. Lester Piggott, riding the Fulke Johnson-Houghton-trained two-year-old Campanologist, looked to have a race sewn up when racing clear inside the final furlong. Only yards from the line the animal swerved, throwing Piggott to the ground. After the stewards had examined the patrol film, they determined the great jockey and his mount had parted company before the finishing line, thus forfeiting the race.

Windsor races have been traditionally popular with boys from Eton College, situated on the opposite side of the river. Illegal visits by the schoolboys have on many occasions been cut short by unfortunate meetings with racegoing members of the teaching staff partaking in a little gambling on their well-earned evenings off. Jakie Astor, the future owner of many flat racers of class, used to swim across the river with his clothes balanced on his head to visit the strictly out-of-bounds racecourse in his days as an Eton boy.

One of the most bizarre of racing moments occurred in the last race at a Windsor summer evening fixture. As the runners ran into the loop at the bottom of the course, the mount of the light-weight jockey Des Cullen ran out of control towards the rails on the bottom bend. Unable to turn at such a pace, the animal ran off the course and landed with an enormous splash in the Mill Stream, which runs close by. Des Cullen, who was unable to swim, was fortunate that one of the ground staff was nearby. He was able to pull the jockey safely from the strong stream, and probably saved Cullen's life. At the subsequent steward's enquiry, the panel were somewhat surprised to interview the brave rider, swathed in a blanket: Cullen was so worried that he might keep the stewards waiting that he thought he had not time enough to change, having discarded his sodden silks and britches.

Windsor has never during its history sought to upgrade its position to become a major track. Its attractive tree-lined paddock and tranquil riverside setting has always attracted the public to its meetings. Race sponsorship has been increased in recent years by the current clerk of the course, Hugo Bevan. Many firms entertain their clients in tents set on the lawns in between the weighing room and the paddock at the regular summer evening fixtures. Windsor would never claim to rival its illustrious Berkshire neighbours, Newbury and Ascot, but the attendance figures and the size of Windsor's fields must be the envy of the managements of many of the country's courses, large and small.

10
THE PERIPHERY OF BERKSHIRE RACING

If the public associate Berkshire's racing industry with her famous trainers and her three racecourses, it is because these aspects of the industry have the highest profile. Constant mention in the newspapers and on television assure that they are always in the public eye. There are a multitude of other facets of the industry which often do not gain the attention they deserve.

The backbone to any successful racing stable is its staff. The great racecourse triumphs can never occur without the round–the–clock attention which the racehorse must have at home. The unsung heroes of the racing stable are the head lads. They are responsible for the running of the trainer's yard during his frequent absences on the racecourse. In the majority of cases they are also responsible for the feeding programmes of the horses, a most vital ingredient in any animal's training schedule. Rarely seen on the country's racecourses, their place is in the less glamorous confines of the stable yard at home.

Ray Laing, Peter Walwyn's head lad in the golden Seven Barrows years of the seventies, was a master of his craft. A marvellous feeder of a horse, Laing believed that when an animal reached peak fitness, its stomach became smaller. He was not a believer in the often–practised method of feeding a fit horse as much as he would eat. Tremendously knowledgeable about the fragile legs of the thoroughbred, he would often prefer to cure ailments in the old fashioned way rather than resort to the use of modern drugs, such as antibiotics. A swollen leg would in many cases be treated with the herb comfrey, wrapped next to the leg in a bandage. The cut or swelling would heal rapidly without the need for any drugs at all. This method was used by the great Letcombe trainer Charles Morton to enable the lame Sunstar to run at Epsom and land the Derby of 1911.

Laing later joined the ranks of Lambourn trainers and had great success. He won two very valuable Irish two-year-old races in the eighties with Roaring Riva and Cameroun before announcing his retirement in 1988.

He could not remain inactive for long. At nearly seventy years of age he renewed his licence in 1991, and trains a small string from his yard on the Hungerford Hill on the outskirts of Lambourn. Laing's successor at Seven Barrows was Matt McCormack, later to train at Major Sneyd's old East Manton stables at Sparsholt near Wantage. McCormack trained the very

Matt McCormack, one of Peter Walwyn's head lads in the 1970s, riding Grundy. McCormack now trains at Sparsholt in Oxfordshire

useful miler Horage, who won the St James's Palace at Ascot in 1983. McCormack experienced a further triumph at the Royal Meeting when he won the Jersey Stakes of 1992 with Prince Ferdinand.

Laing had some distinguished head lad colleagues in Lambourn in the seventies. Peter Gomez was Peter Nelson's head lad for many years. Snow Knight's Derby victory of 1974 brought Gomez's much deserved recognition in the twilight of his career. Longstanding partnerships between head lad and trainer are often an important feature of the most successful yards. Brian Delaney was Fred Winter's head lad from the outset and remains in the same capacity with Winter's successor Charlie Brooks. Corky Brown has similarly been Nick Henderson's head lad since Henderson first received his licence. Geordie Campbell has served Dick Hern's yard as head lad for many years. Eric Wheeler, previously Jack Colling's head man at Ilsley, was Stan Mellor's head lad at Linkslade before branching out on his own in a small yard behind Mellor's old stables. Wheeler has won some good races in his relatively short training career with the good old sprint handicapper, Green Dollar.

When the horses leave their home stables to take up their racecourse engagements, the travelling head lad assumes responsibility. The doyen of travelling lads was Buster Haslam, who travelled the West Ilsley horses of

Buster Haslam, Dick Hern's famous travelling head lad, walking on the left of Nashwan and Willie Carson

Jack Colling and Dick Hern for many years. Haslam was a familiar figure to all racegoers, as he supervised the many great successes the Hodcott yard had in his time. The immaculate way his charges were turned out on every occasion made it possible to spot a Hern runner with ease in the paddock: a racecard was not needed to facilitate identification. The racing world suffered a great loss when Buster Haslam took his own life a few years ago. It seems strange to see a Hern runner without Haslam walking unobtrusively by its side, ready for any pre-race eventuality. Tony Driscoll is another familiar racecourse face. He has travelled Peter Walwyn's horses ever since the trainer started. Driscoll served his time at Hodcott in Jack Colling's day and learnt much of his craft from Buster Haslam. Experienced travelling lads are vital to the modern racing yard, as nowadays the good-class horse is more and more campaigned abroad, often staying some days away from home.

Another vital component of any successful yard is the work rider. Experienced judges of home gallops are a major asset for any trainer. As well as knowing intuitively the right pace to go, the experienced work rider will spot the slightest sign if his mount is not performing up to scratch. Tommy Jennings, the former jockey, has been an integral part of Paul Cole's set up for many years. As the trainer's leading work rider, his views on whether an animal is ready for a race or at the top of his form at home are an important part of the trainer's future race planning. Jennings rode Generous after his Arc de Triomphe failure in a searching gallop at Whatcombe. He reported that the horse was not giving him the same feel as earlier in the season. The horse forfeited his next engagement and never ran again. Brian Proctor, a former Gordon Richards apprentice, rode in all the important gallops during Dick Hern's time at Ilsley. Many difficult horses have been taught to put their best foot forward by Proctor. His judgement of a piece of work is famous for its accuracy. He predicted that the relatively unfancied Petoski would win the 1985 King George after a good gallop at Ilsley. He was later proved to be entirely correct in his assumption.

The right blend of force and kindness in teaching young horses the rudiments of galloping is a vital component of the work rider's art. Often he will report a horse too weak to be moving at fast paces. The trainer, digesting this information, can then give the animal more time. Conversely he can feel if an animal is lazy and not showing his true colours in the morning gallops. More forceful riding will soon teach the horse his job and make him fit enough for a racecourse appearance. Darkie Deacon was entrusted to teach the tearaway jumper The Dikler to learn to settle. So successful was Deacon in performing this task that the horse was to become a future Cheltenham Gold Cup winner for Fulke Walwyn's Lambourn stable.

The steep Berkshire downs test the work rider to the full. Gallops are never ridden at full tilt because of the nature of the terrain. The Berkshire work rider must judge a horse's capabilities without often galloping him at maximum speed. It is by no means an easy task to assess a horse at less than racing pace: the work rider's experience alone can answer him this question.

There is no doubt that most stable staff enter the racing industry with the ambition to become a jockey. Nowadays both sexes can ride under rules: the stable lass can therefore harbour the same ambition as her male counterpart. The fact is that few attain their original dream. The majority, either because of increasing weight or lack of race riding talent, are destined to be stable lads or lasses for their racing lives. However, the position should not be demeaned. The care and attention which they lavish on the horses entrusted to their care can often be a vital ingredient in subsequent racecourse success. See You Then, Nick Henderson's triple Champion Hurdler, was so difficult in his box that only his lad, the former George Todd apprentice, Glyn Foster, could handle him. His trainer was unable to enter the box without See You Then attempting to savage him. The stable lad knows his individual horses more intimately than anybody else. Often he alone can detect a difference in the animal's behaviour in the stable, which indicates that the animal is below par and consequently unlikely to show top form.

Several top riders have served their apprenticeships in Berkshire stables. The fine flat jockey Frederick Allsopp was apprenticed to the Lambourn Place trainer James Humphreys in the 1880s. He was later to win the Derby on Lord Bradford's Sir Hugo in 1892. Another fine Victorian jockey was Luke Snowden. He was apprenticed to Joseph Saxon in Lambourn. He won the 1861 Oaks on Brown Duchess for the Saxon stable, and also two St Legers, on Sunbeam in 1858 and St Albans in 1860. He was second in the Leger on the Seven Barrows-trained Kettledrum in 1861. A year later at the tender age of twenty-two Snowden died and was buried in Lambourn churchyard. Fred Templeman, later to train three Classic winners from the Meridian stables in Lambourn, was apprenticed

Frederick Allsopp, a fine flat rider at the turn of the century. He was apprenticed to the Lamborne Place trainer James Humphreys, and won the 1892 Derby on Sir Hugo

there to John Hallick. Templeman, who rode the 1919 Derby winner Grand Parade, later took over Hallick's stable when the trainer died in 1921.

In more modern times Lester Piggott learnt the rudiments of his craft from his father Keith at South Bank stables, now the property of Barry Hills. Hills has continued the South Bank tradition in producing top riders. His twin sons, Richard and Michael, learnt to ride the thoroughbred at an early age on the Faringdon Road gallops, which their father used. Also apprenticed to Barry Hills was the leading flat race jockey Ray Cochrane, who won nine races on the fast two-year-old filly Nagwa during his time with Hills. Increasing weight forced Cochrane to go jumping for a time, riding for the Lambourn trainer Duncan Sasse. A serious fall strangely caused him to lose weight again. Resuming his career with Barry Hills's former assistant Ron Sheather, Cochrane scored several big race successes on Chief Singer. Now he is regularly among the top five jockeys in the land. At present Barry Hills employs the former champion apprentice Darryl Holland, who started his riding career at Manton and moved back to South Bank with Barry Hills.

Paul Cole produced three leading apprentices while training from Hill House, Lambourn. Although David Dineley and Robert Edmondson did not manage the transition to the senior ranks, Richard Quinn improved.

Still riding for Cole's Whatcombe stable, he is now one of the leading flat riders in the country. In the sixties Doug Marks also produced some top-class apprentices. David Yates, who won the Cesarewitch on Golden Fire and Peter Madden, who used to partner the good sprinter Fireside Chat, served their time with Marks.

On the jumping front the former champion rider Jack Dowdeswell served his apprenticeship with Ted Gwilt, Fulke Walwyn's predecessor at Saxon House. John Francome was with Fred Winter for all his racing career. Another rider to rise through the ranks to become a successful jockey was Ally Branford, who rode many winners in the Queen Mother's colours in the late sixties and early seventies for his employer, Fulke Walwyn.

Another figure crucial to the training of the racehorse is the gallop-man. His responsibility is to keep the training grounds mown, harrowed and rolled to ensure an even surface for the fragile legs of the thoroughbred to exercise on safely. He must keep the training areas free of mole hills and runs, which can break a leg if encountered at speed. 'Putting back' of gallops cut to ribbons by a multitude of hooves on rain-sodden ground is no easy task. If reparation is left until the weather is too dry, rough ground will be the result. If 'put back' in wet weather with machinery, the gallop may suffer untold damage. In winter, often the gallopman must be aboard his tractor in the hours of darkness, ensuring a frost-free all-weather surface for the jumpers the next day.

Eddie Fisher has supervised the public gallops in Lambourn for many years. Many trainers, whatever their standing, have suffered the full force of Fisher's tongue, if caught using an unmarked bit of ground. Fisher's knowledge of matters pertaining to gallops is such that many trainers seek his advice about their own private working grounds. When Peter Walwyn moved to Seven Barrows in the sixties, a plague of moles badly affected the famous Faringdon Road turf, so he requested Fisher's help. The Lambourn gallopman had to set his traps long distances from the gallops to rid the area completely of the racehorse's greatest enemy. It says much for Fisher's skill that the turf was restored to its former excellence rapidly: mole damage has never been a problem since.

Many other businesses serve Berkshire's large racing industry. Two veterinary practices are based in Lambourn itself. The firm of Blackman O'Gorman, based in Newbury, is also patronized by many Berkshire studs and stables. The Ridgeway Veterinary group has been established in

Eddie Fisher – the Lambourn
gallop man

Lambourn for many years and was the sole practice in the village until
recently. Barry Park, who practised from Lockinge for some years, having
previously worked for the Ridgeway group, saw the need for a modern
veterinary hospital in Lambourn with full operating and bloodtesting
facilities. Previously serious cases had often to travel either to Bristol or
Newmarket. Blood which required anything but the least detailed analysis were also sent to Newmarket. Park built and designed a hospital,
incorporating within it highly sophisticated blood reading facilities. As
a result serious injuries can now be treated on the doorstep of any Lambourn trainer's yard. Because of Park's new veterinary hospital, the
facilities in Lambourn now match those of her sister training centre,
Newmarket. The practice which he formed, Valley Equine, is now firmly
established at its new Lambourn base.

John Gray, who practised for many years in the area first with the
Ridgeway Group in Lambourn and later in partnership with Barry Park
at Lockinge, recalled an interesting moment in his early career. Just qualified and green as grass, he could not understand why he was given the
task of identifying a dead horse at an East Ilsley stables he had never
before set foot in. Only later did he learn that the dead horse was believed to be the real Francascal, who had vanished after a ringer had
replaced him to land a massive coup in a Bath seller. Gray always believed

that his senior and, at that time, more qualified colleagues were frightened what would happen to them if they identified the animal as Francascal. Hence they left the dangerous task to their much younger colleague!

Each racing stable employs its own blacksmith, who must plate the animal in lighter shoes for racing, reshoe it with heavier exercise shoes when it has run, and generally deal with any injury which involves the foot. A blacksmith is a permanent fixture at any racing yard or race-course: a twisted or lost front shoe can lose a vital day's exercise or a racetrack run. Consequently the blacksmith must be on hand at every moment. Tony Hailstone, a famous Lambourn farrier, was once plating an animal in the quiet of the afternoon. Suddenly his back seized up (a common problem which nearly all blacksmiths encounter in their career) and Hailstone could not move. He screamed and shouted for help but all the stable staff were absent for the afternoon. As the hours passed by, the inmate of the box, a rather quarrelsome young colt began to tire of Hailstone's company and to the farrier's horror began to rear up and kick out. In the nick of time the head lad arrived back for evening stables. Hearing the blacksmith's frenzied shouts, he dragged him out of the furious colt's box. Hailstone always believed he was only minutes from an unfortunate end, a helpless target for the ill-tempered young colt.

Many other businesses have the racing industry as their principal client. The Lambourn racing saddler, E.J. Wicks, has been established in the village since the turn of the century. As well as selling tack, they run a vitally important repair service. Bridles, saddles, rugs and sheets are patched up again and again to prolong their life. Such is the expense of saddlery today that most trainers are reluctant to purchase new gear if repairs are possible. Wicks sells all the accoutrements which the modern racehorse and rider requires, and also runs a collection and delivery service around the outlying Berkshire yards. The famous East Ilsley saddler, Stan Ward, no longer trades. Local trainers used to have a field day there when the powerful West Ilsley yard of Dick Hern replaced old tack. Hern's second-hand gear was far superior to their ancient tack, and often it was cheaper for trainers to buy Hern's discarded saddlery than to repair their own.

Firms who provide forage and fodder for horses count the racing industry as a major client. The horse food firm of Dodson and Horrell now has a depot in Lambourn to service its many clients efficiently. The old established Blunsdon firm of Toomers also provides the racing fraternity with corn, nuts and bran. Straw and hay dealers number trainers and studs among their most valued clients, as do the distributors of horse bedding (straw, paper or shavings). Purveyors of food supplements, blood tonics and veterinary remedies are regular visitors to the county's yards. Racehorses require the best of feed and hay to perform at the highest level: no corners can be cut in these departments. Scientifically mixed and blended feeds are now a feature of the modern racehorse's training diet. Those firms who do not move with the times soon do not number the racing fraternity among their clients.

Horse transport is another business directly dependent on the racing community. In 1930 Hugh Nugent realized the motorized horse box would soon replace the train as the means of horse transport. He soon assembled a fleet of horse boxes to transport Berkshire horses to the race meetings around the country. The firm, later to be named Lambourn Ridgeway Transport, had a virtual monopoly of the area's business. Rising transport prices and the design and development of the small two-horse box, which did not require a specially licensed driver, saw many trainers purchase their own boxes. Lambourn Transport lost much business as a result of this change. In the eighties the Nugent family sold the firm. In 1992 it again changed hands and is now the property of the former Lambourn trainer, Merrick Francis, son of the former royal jockey and distinguished author, Dick Francis.

Another Berkshire transport operator is the former Lambourn and Newmarket trainer Michael Hinchliffe. Hinchliffe knows the routes to the country's racecourses better than most. He was Lester Piggott's personal driver for some fifteen years when the rider was champion jockey on many occasions. The former champion jump jockey Bryan Marshall ran a horse transport firm, Compton Transport, based in the village of that name, until his recent death. One of Marshall's principal clients was the powerful flat yard of Dick Hern from nearby West Ilsley.

The Yorkshire firm of auctioneers, Botterills, run Berkshire's only horse sales. Selling at a ring adjacent to the Ascot racecourse stables, they run many sales throughout the year. Traditionally a dispersal ground for the more moderate racehorse, the firm has upgraded its June Sale, which attracts some good jumping sorts these days. For a few years recently, the firm ran a breeze up sale for two-year-olds. This practice has now been discontinued. Originally started in 1946 at the now defunct Royal Ascot

Hotel by the late Jack Botterill, the firm sold at a site near Winkfield for many years until moving to its present ring at the Ascot racecourse stables. The Botterills have developed Ascot Sales to accommodate those people who do not wish to incur the greater expense of selling at the more traditional venues of Doncaster and Newmarket. As a result of this policy, Ascot Sales is consistently well patronized. In the last decade the firm has had the distinction of selling three Grand National winners in the ring, Ben Nevis, Maori Venture and Aldaniti. In 1990 the firm gained their record sale price for a horse-in-training when Sober Mind was knocked down for 85,000 gns.

The British Bloodstock Agency now maintains an office in Lambourn. Having dispensed with its long established London premises to avoid rising costs, the famous agency now has two directors based in Lambourn, the rest operate from Newmarket. Johnny Lewis, who handles the racing interests of the Saudi Prince A. Faisal is one of the Lambourn based directors. The other is Sir Philip Payne-Gallwey, who for many years was the racing manager and bloodstock advisor to the Greek shipping millionaire, Stavros Niarchos. Other Berkshire based bloodstock agents are Lord Patrick Beresford, who operates from Binfield near Ascot and is the Duke of Devonshire's bloodstock advisor, and Julian Lewis of East Garston, who has for many years specialized in the French market. Lewis handled the sale as a stallion of the fine Peter Walwyn-trained miler of the seventies, Free State.

The two racing papers, the *Racing Post* and the *Sporting Life*, employ two reporters specifically to cover the Lambourn and Berkshire training areas. Nick Deacon, son of The Dikler's work rider, Darkie Deacon, is the *Sporting Life's* Lambourn correspondent and his counterpart on the *Racing Post* is Neil Morrice. These correspondents find the trainers of the modern day generally more open than their predecessors, the Rodbourne family, the famous family of work-watchers, did in the past. Michael Phillips, Mandarin of *The Times*, is another racing journalist, who has lived in the Lambourn area for many years. Phillips utilized a family connection with Peter Walwyn's wife, Bonk, to tip many winners, as a result of inside information gained by early morning gallop-watching in the Walwyn stable's golden years. In recent times, the form book publishers Raceform have moved from their old Curzon Street base to the training village of Compton. All compilation and distribution is now conducted from their Berkshire base.

Jimmy Lindley, the former top flat rider and current BBC racing commentator, is also a long-time Berkshire resident. He has lived at Speen near Newbury for many years. Some years ago Lindley managed the horses of the major owner, Mrs Mullion, who numbered the Leger winner Ragusa among her many good horses. One morning while watching her string exercise, Lindley turned to Mrs Mullion. Waxing lyrical, he said that he believed there could be no more pleasant place on earth than the downs on a beautiful summer's morning. The former jockey was somewhat taken aback when Mrs Mullion replied that she would be more inclined to agree with him if he extinguished the large cigar he was smoking with great relish, at that early stage of the morning.

The Jockeys Association is also Berkshire based, with its office in Newbury. Created in the sixties to look after the jockeys' interests and argue their case, the current secretary is a High Court judge's son, Michael Caulfield. The two joint Presidents of the Association are Dr Devious's Derby winning rider, John Reid and the champion jump jockey, Peter Scudamore. The Jockeys Association has developed into an important racing industry pressure group. Currently it is preparing for its biggest test. The Association will be responsible for ensuring that the transition to a system of compulsory overnight declaration of jockeys runs smoothly. Its office will be the communications centre for the new venture.

Henry Ponsonby, one of the leading racing syndicate operators, runs his business from the village of Chaddleworth in Berkshire. Ponsonby advertises in the national press on a huge scale to find shareholders for the various horses he has in training. Multiple ownership of horses is possible under the Rules of Racing if a club is formed. In 1992 Ponsonby formed the Generous Club, named after the Whatcombe Derby winner of 1991. Club members purchase an interest in several animals prepared by the trainer of Generous, Paul Cole, for the sum of £595. The benefit of th club system of ownership is that the subscriber has several strings to his bow for a relatively cheap investment. Ponsonby and his syndicates have patronized Paul Cole's stable for many years. Many people who could not otherwise afford to own horses have been brought into racing as a result of syndicated ownership. Ponsonby keeps his huge variety of owners and shareholders informed by regular newsletters and telephone information lines, which are for the exclusive use of his syndicates or clubs. The recession has hit syndication, like the rest of the industry, hard. Ponsonby

Henry Ponsonby – one of racing's leading
syndicate managers

has found 1992 the most difficult year of his whole career to find clients
for his various horses.

Various livery stables dotted around the county are patronized by trainers to break in their young stock and complete their early conditioning
work. Many trainers like to send horses to such establishments for a mid-
season break, just for a change of scenery. Many livery yard proprietors
supplement their incomes by training and qualifying point-to-pointers.
John Porter runs such an establishment at Berkeley House, Lambourn.
Porter also has a horse jacuzzi, which is patronized by many local trainers
to ease the pain on the tired or injured limbs and muscles of their
charges. The livery stable proprietors' business tends to thrive when
trainers' yards are full. In recessive times their business suffers as trainers,
who are short of horses, must for economic reasons keep their own yards
as full as they can.

The BBC racing drama series *Trainer* is filmed at Compton. The stable
used is the famous Hamilton House yard from where George Beeby sent
Brendan's Nephew and Silver Fame to win two Cheltenham Gold Cups
in the years around the Second World War. The training grounds used in
the series are the famous Compton gallops owned by the Cundell family.
Peter Cundell is the programme's racing advisor and trains the horses
which appear in the film. *Trainer*, if not attracting vast viewing figures

during its first season, has been given a vote of confidence by the BBC, as a new series is being filmed to go out in the autumn of 1992. The publicity which the series has given to the Berkshire training grounds can do the county's racing industry nothing but good. A criticism levelled at the programme is that the star and trainer in the series, Mike Hardy, played by Mark Greenstreet, appears to lack a sense of humour. Those who pursue this high risk career in the real world would soon become insane without one.

The firms which provide the yards and studs with their horse feed and hay need a buoyant racing industry to thrive. The same is true for the providers of horse bedding (straw, shavings or paper), the vets, the farriers, the transport operators, the syndicate managers or the saddlers. It is a question of supply and demand. The more horses there are trained or reared in Berkshire, the more business the many firms on the periphery of the industry obtain. The recession has affected the amount of horses in training throughout the country. Consequently businesses directly or indirectly involved with the racing industry have suffered accordingly. Berkshire in this respect is not alone in needing economic recovery rapidly.

11
BERKSHIRE STUDS

As the 1974 county boundary changes deprived Berkshire of the training villages situated north of the Ridgeway, she also lost some famous studs as a result. Aston Upthorpe, now the property of Sheikh Ahmed al Maktoum and the home of the former King George winner, the stallion Mtoto, is located near Didcot and is now part of Oxfordshire. The famous Hardwick Stud, where Cyllene was born as long ago as 1895 and where Lester Piggott's first Derby winner, Never Say Die, was reared and weaned, is also now part of Oxfordshire. Now no longer used as a thoroughbred stud, its paddocks lie to the north of the Thames, near Whitchurch, just across the river from Pangbourne. The Lockinge Stud, where Christopher Loyd stood Decoy Boy and King of Spain, is similarly now in Oxfordshire. The stud is situated on the part of the Lockinge estate which lies to the north of the Ridgeway.

Other famous studs cannot be claimed by Berkshire, although they boast Berkshire postal addresses. To the south Highclere, where Blenheim, the 1930 Derby winner was bred and where Queen's Hussar, the father of Brigadier Gerard stood, is the property of the Queen's racing manager Lord Carnarvon, and lies in Hampshire, a few miles south of Newbury alongside the A34. A near neighbour to Highclere is the famous Gainsborough Stud, now the property of Maktoum al Maktoum. Gainsborough, named after the 1918 triple crown winner bred there by Lady James Douglas, was once owned by the racehorse owner and Beckhampton trainer, Herbert Blagrave. Still run by Blagrave's stud manager, Michael Goodbody, Gainsborough has been much modernized since Maktoum al Maktoum became its owner. It is situated in the village of Woolton Hill, just across the county border line in Hampshire.

Another Hampshire stud which carries a Berkshire postal address is Woolton House, also in the village of Woolton Hill. Here the Hue-Williams family bred many top-class horses, including Supreme Court, the 1971 1,000 Guineas and Oaks heroine Altesse Royale, and the good stayer Rock Roi, who unluckily lost two Ascot Gold Cups on disqualifications.

Even closer to the border, although just in Hampshire, is the Woodhaven stud at East Woodhay. Here John and Jean Hislop bred one of the greatest horses ever trained in Berkshire, the peerless Brigadier Gerard. The stud is now owned by John Moreton and Juliet Reed. Miss Reed owned the 1988 Grand National winner Rhyme and Reason. Another stud in the same area on the Hampshire side of the county border is Heatherwold. A mile or so north of Highclere stud on the opposite side of the A34, Heatherwold bred the 1990 Arc de Triomphe winner, Saumarez.

Just across the Thames near Taplow lies the famous Cliveden Stud. The Thames serves here as the county boundary. In this case Buckinghamshire can claim the credit, not Berkshire. Cliveden was purchased in 1966 on the death of the third Lord Astor by Louis Freedman. Mr Freedman achieved his lifetime's ambition when he won the 1987 Derby with the home-bred Reference Point, sadly to die recently in the early stages of his stallion career.

Although these famous studs lie just outside Berkshire's county boundaries, within the limits are other breeding establishments of renown. In the west the Kingwood Stud, situated next to Dick Hern's newly constructed Kingwood stables, lies at the top of Hungerford Hill, a mile towards the motorway from the village of Lambourn. Kingwood Stud was previously the Lambourn Stud, bought in 1924 by the Lambourn trainer Ossie Bell in partnership with his principal owner Sir Hugo Cunliffe-Owen. The winner of the 1928 Derby, Felstead, owned by Sir Hugo and trained by Bell in the village of Lambourn, was one of the first foals ever to be born on the Lambourn Stud. Bell purchased his dam Felkington at the 1924 December Sales for 2,100 gns. Felstead never ran after his Derby triumph. He was retired to stand at the Lambourn Stud and started covering in the 1930 season. He remained there until his death in 1946.

Felstead sired the filly Rockfel, who won the 1938 1,000 Guineas, Oaks and Champion Stakes for Hugo Cunliffe-Owen. Sadly she was only to produce one foal before her death in 1941 from a twisted gut. The foal was Rockfella. Trained like his mother Rockfel by Ossie Bell, Rockfella was to prove a fine stallion. Sent to stud at the end of his three-year-old career, Bell and Cunliffe-Owen stood him in place of the now dead Felstead at Lambourn Stud. He sired the 2,000 Guineas winner Rockavon, and the winner of the Irish equivalent Linacre during his time at stud.

When Ossie Bell died in 1949, his widow Renée formed a partnership with Wyndam Torr under the name of Lambourn Stud Limited. Wyndam Torr was lucky enough to make an inspired purchase. He bought the mare Chambiges from Edward Somerset for only 1,000 gns. Somerset had purchased Chambiges for only 85 gns at the 1958 Newmarket Houghton Sales. Falling ill, Somerset decided to sell at a profit, having secured a nomination to Rockefella, the Lambourn Stud stallion. Covered by Rockefella for three seasons in a row, Chambiges proved to be a bargain. She produced the fine staying filly Outcrop, trained at Newmarket by Geoffrey Barling, the dam of Sharpen Up, Rochetta and Riches, the dam of Richboy. The Lambourn Stud bred another top-class filly in 1958. Cynara won the 1960 Queen Mary for Gerry Oldham. Trained at Newmarket by Harry Wragg, she was later to prove a fine broodmare for Oldham, producing the Prix Lupin winner Stintino and the 1982 2,000 Guineas winner Zino.

In 1969 Mrs Bell moved to Faringdon. Establishing a stud there, she kept the name Lambourn Stud. The new purchasers of the former Lambourn Stud renamed it Kingwood, the title it retains to this day. Since Mrs Bell's move, the stud has changed ownership several times. The Arrowsmith-Browns were Mrs Bell's immediate successors and stood the French horse Klairon there. In the seventies the stud changed hands three times. The former Newmarket trainer Tim Hollowell stood the stallion Doon there. His successors were a Spanish consortium, who in turn sold the premises to Mr and Mrs Terence Vigors. Previously based in County Carlow in Ireland, the Vigors family purchased the stud in 1979. Since 1985 Fiona Vigors, the wife of Terence Vigors's son Nicky, the Jockey Club starter and former Lambourn trainer, has managed the stud.

Fiona Vigors, the daughter of the distinguished Epsom-based blood-stock agent and vet, the late George Forbes, has a formidable record with animals purchased as foals to resell as yearlings. She bought those fast horses Gallic League and Rock City as foals to resell. Also reared at Kingwood was the 1991 King's Stand winner Elbio. The stud now specializes in preparing yearlings for sale. As well as playing host to a band of boarding broodmares, Kingwood is most popular with trainers in the area, who send their horses for a change of routine and scenery to the nearby stud.

Until recently, Fiona Vigors's mother, Joan Forbes, ran the Burley Lodge Stud at Beenham near Reading. Mrs Forbes stood the stallions

Derrylin and the Derby winner Relko at the stud's former location at Shinfield.

South of Lambourn is the Benham Stud, at Marsh Benham in between Hungerford and Newbury. Managed by the East Garton farmer Roger Denton, the stud was established on land leased from the estate of Sir Richard Sutton in 1950. One mare, Port Beam, a gift from the former West Ilsley trainer Eric Stedall, was the only resident in those early days. Since then the stud has at varied times been home to the stallions Runnymede, Queen's Hussar, after he had left Highclere, and Streak. The present stallions resident at Benham are Beveled, who arrived in 1988 and Ballacashtal, a noted sire of fast two-year-olds, who arrived in 1984. Among the decent horses Benham has bred was the fast Bill Marshall-trained two-year-old Legal Eagle, who won the 1974 Richmond Stakes at Goodwood.

Further west is Lord Howard de Walden's Berkshire home at Avington, near Hungerford. On his estates is the Templeton stud, where his yearlings are sent to take advantage of the summer grass of the paddocks, which lie above the water meadows of the River Kennet. Lord Howard's champion miler Kris and Derby winner Slip Anchor spent their yearling summer in Templeton's tranquil surroundings. Lord Howard de Walden is one of the last successful British owner breeders left. Successes in his famous apricot colours are always well received. The sporting owner experienced two triumphs at the 1992 Royal Ascot meeting.

Across the Kennet beyond Kintbury at West Woodhay is the home of John Henderson, a fellow Jockey Club member of Lord Howard de Walden and father of the Lambourn trainer Nicky Henderson. Never having more than one or two mares, Henderson has bred some good winners at West Woodhay. From his mare Acclio he bred the useful handicapper of the seventies, Acquaint, a good dual purpose horse, who won the Imperial Cup over hurdles and the good sprinter, Acquit, who won the 1969 Albemarle Stakes at Ascot. One of the last of Acclio's progeny was the winning 1975 two-year-old filly Acquire, by Burglar. Trained at Seven Barrows by Peter Walwyn, she was retired to stud at the end of her two-year-old year. Back at the knee, she proved that, for racing or breeding, confirmation is not everything. Her second foal was the speedy filly Chellaston Park, who won five races as a two-year-old in 1981 for Bruce Hobbs's Newmarket stable. As a three-year-old, Chellaston Park became one of the leading sprinters of her generation, finishing second in the King's Stand, the Temple and the William Hill Sprint Championship at York. Although Henderson sold Acquire and her Record Token filly foal, later to become Chellaston Park, at the 1979 December Sales for a combined price of just over 3,000 gns, he had the satisfaction of breeding one of the fastest fillies of recent years at his West Woodhay stud.

At Chieveley, a few miles north of Newbury, is the Chieveley Manor Stud of another Jockey Club member Christopher Spence. Reopened in 1984, Spence has since bred the useful mare Sesame, who won the St Simon Stakes at Newbury. Trained by Spence's brother-in-law David Morley at Newmarket, Sesame is the best horse Spence has owned since Frontier Goddess, who won the Yorkshire Oaks of 1969 for Peter Walwyn's Lambourn stable. Further north is the Fawley Stud. On the opposite side of the valley to Whatcombe's famous Woolley Down gallops, Fawley was founded in 1957 by Ian Muir. The first notable horse bred at Fawley was the Cheltenham Gold Cup winner What a Myth. Purchased from Ian Muir as an unbroken three-year-old for only £400 by Ryan Price, What a Myth was by Muir's first stallion Coup de Myth out of What a Din. Muir's partnership with the Honner family produced some tremendous Fawley-bred stock. Grandpa's Legacy was a fine racemare bred there. Later, after retiring to the paddocks, she was to produce the good Peter Walwyn-trained Reliance horse Consol, who won the Geoffrey Freer Stakes at Newbury in 1975. More recently the stud bred the good stayer Destroyer. Trained at Lambourn by Kim Brassey, he won the Henry II Stakes at Sandown before finishing second in the Ascot Gold Cup of 1985.

Among the stallions which have stood at Fawley are the great stayer Buckskin, the good miler, Track Spare and Supreme Sovereign. Supreme Sovereign was a savage, but fortunately he was also a hydrophobic and a well-directed hosepipe was often the safest way to persuade the stallion to return to his box after covering a mare. The former Henry Cecil-trained Faustus is now the resident stallion at Fawley Stud. Recently the Muirs took delivery of the stallion Northern Game. Another stallion with a reputation as a savage, the Muirs have quickly found the key to Northern Game and he is covering his mares without a problem at the present. In the eighties Ian Muir sold Fawley to the bookmaking firm Esal Commodities, who owned many horses at the time. When Esal went broke, the stud was bought by Mr and Mrs D.J. Deer. Ian Muir manages the stud for them.

Near Wokingham is the Ewar Farm Stud of the Richards family. A large stud of some 500 acres, Ewar has over the years bred a number of good class animals. Founded in 1964 by the chartered accountant Tony Richards, the stud bred the Royal Hunt Cup winner of 1978 Fear Naught. Standaan, who won the Stewards Cup in 1979 was also bred there. Richards also owns a French stud, the Haras de la Pomme, which he acquired in 1974: the Richards family like to race on an international scale. Richards's Bold Arrangement finished second in the Kentucky Derby for Clive Brittain's Newmarket stable. He also patronizes the French stables of John Hammond and Andre Fabre. As well as retaining animals to race in their own colours, the Richards sell their stock at Newmarket and at Deauville. Twice Ewar Farm-bred yearlings have reached the magic 100,000 gns sale price in the ring. Richards has a few horses trained at his Wokingham home by his stud groom, Cliff Austin. Whippet, a good sprinter of recent times, was trained there for a time. Richards also patronized the Lambourn stable of Dave Hanley. Hanley won the Cambridgeshire with Lottogift in 1975. Lottogift carried the colours of Tony Richards's wife, Emily.

The county's *pièce de résistance* is the Saudi Prince Khaled Abdullah's Juddmonte Farms near Wargrave-on-Thames. The present stud is the flagship of the enormous breeding operation Abdullah runs in this country.

Mares and foals at Khaled Abdullah's showpiece Juddmonte Farms. The stud is situated near Wargrave

Also under the Juddmonte banner are two Newmarket studs, Eagle Lane and Banstead Manor. In Ireland Juddmonte Farms has two studs, Ferrans in Co. Meath and New Abbey in Co. Kildare. In the United States there are no less than three studs in Kentucky. Nowadays Abdullah owns over 150 mares. At the last count he was reported to have some 230 horses in training with Roger Charlton, Guy Harwood, Barry Hills, John Gosden and Henry Cecil in England, and with Andre Fabre in Paris.

Originally purchased in 1979 from the breeder Gerard Leigh, the stud was known as Cayton Park. Before Leigh's time, the stud had been the property of Mrs Gerald Trimmer-Thompson. She had at one time stood March Past at Cayton Park: March Past had been owned as a racehorse by Mrs Trimmer-Thompson. He was trained at Compton by Ken Cundell and won the Greenham and the Wokingham at Royal Ascot, during a racing career which spanned three seasons. The best horses March Past sired were Queen's Hussar and the useful sprinter Constans, who was trained at Beckhampton by Jeremy Tree. In 1973 Gerard Leigh bought Cayton Park. In time he had assembled a very select group of high-class brood mares. By 1979 Green Girl and Miss Petard were among them. James Delahooke, the leading bloodstock agent, had been retained by Leigh as his stud manager and advisor at Cayton Park. In the summer of 1979 Leigh sold Cayton Park to Abdullah along with five mares, among whom was Miss Petard. In August Delahooke was appointed as Abdullah's racing manager and the new acquisition of Cayton Park became his overall responsibility.

In 1980 Abdullah won his first Classic when the Jeremy Tree-trained colt Known Fact was awarded the 2,000 Guineas after Nureyev's disqualification. In 1982 Abdullah gained his first success as a breeder when Fine Edge won at Newmarket's Guineas meeting. A year earlier the old Cayton Park Stud had been totally renovated to become the public side of the Berkshire operation. Known Fact was installed as the resident stallion. A former dairy farm was purchased next door to house Abdullah's rapidly increasing band of brood mares. Both properties were developed and designed by James Delahooke. When they were finished at the end of 1981, Juddmonte was the most sophisticated stud of the time.

Delahooke, as well as purchasing many top-class mares for Abdullah, bought him two colts at Keenland Sales in 1982 and 1984, who were to prove of the highest class. The 1982 purchase Rainbow Quest won the

The stud buildings at Juddmonte

Arc de Triomphe, as did the 1984 purchase Dancing Brave. In 1985 Delahooke and Abdullah parted company. The operation at Wargrave was then taken over by Tony Chapman, who ran the Abdullah racing interests until October 1988. During Chapman's tenure, the two New-market studs were purchased. Since 1988 Philip Mitchell has been Juddmonte's general manager. Mitchell previously ran Lord Hartington's Newmarket stud, Side Hill, as well as the Brook Stud.

In 1990 the huge investment Abdullah had placed in his breeding operation of Juddmonte Farms came to fruition. He won the Epsom Derby with Quest for Fame and the French equivalent with Sanglamore, both trained at Beckhampton by the first season trainer Roger Charlton, who had taken over Jeremy Tree's Beckhampton yard. The Juddmonte-bred Deploy, also handled by Charlton, narrowly failed to complete an unbelievable treble, finishing second in the Irish Derby. In 1991 Juddmonte had further Classic success when the French-trained Toulon won the St Leger.

The Arc winner Rainbow Quest stood as a stallion at Wargrave for the seasons of 1986 and 1987 before moving to Abdullah's Newmarket stud of Banstead Manor to join the fine miler Warning. Warning was a son of the first Juddmonte stallion Known Fact. Rainbow Quest, as well as siring Abdullah's Epsom Derby winner, Quest for Fame, is also the sire of the Arc winner Saumarez.

The establishment at Wargrave is now used almost exclusively as Khaled Abdullah's private stud: so great is the number of mares he now owns. One of the largest owners on the turf, Abdullah's acquisition and development of the branch of Juddmonte Farms at Wargrave was a major boost for the Berkshire racing industry. His commitment to British racing appears to be as strong as ever. The band of broodmares currently lodging on Berkshire soil must be the most valuable group of mares ever assembled on one stud.

Other establishments within the county are now no longer active studs. Wyld Court, near the training village of Compton, was for many years a renowned breeding establishment. Founded in 1913 by Sir William Cooke, Wyld Court bred the 1946 2,000 Guineas winner, Happy Knight. His brother, Happy Landing, was third in the 1944 Derby, having been sold previously as a horse-in-training for the then substantial figure of 13,500 gns. Happy Knight's first ever victory was in the 2,000 Guineas. Trained by Henri Jelliss at Newmarket, he won easily by four lengths in the hands of Tommy Weston. Transferred to George Todd's stable at the end of the season without another win under his belt, he did not win again for Sir William Cooke until his five-year-old year. The long cold winter of 1945 may have been responsible for Happy Knight's Guineas win: many of the leading three-year-olds were still unfit on Guineas day. Sir William Cooke also bred the Doncaster Cup winner Devizes and Hera, who won the Wokingham at Royal Ascot. In 1961 Sir William sold Wyld Court to Mary Marshall, wife of the former Champion jump rider, Bryan Marshall. In 1964 Sir William died at the ripe old age of ninety-two.

Mary Marshall modernized the stud and notably improved the facilities. In 1974 the entrepreneur Peter de Savary and his partners bought the stud. Dave Dick, the former steeplechase jockey, managed Wyld Court. Dick also retained a similar position at Aston Upthorpe, which was at that time the property of the ex-amateur rider, Sir William Piggott-Brown. Lorenzaccio, who beat Nijinsky in the 1970 Champion Stakes, stood at Wyld Court under Dave Dick's management. Early in 1979 Wyld Court was sold to the Green Shield stamp heir, R.S. Tompkins, who leased the stud to Chris Watkins, a former manager of the Hue-Williams stud of Woolton House. In the early eighties, Watkins left Wyld Court for Dorset. During his brief stay, he stood the stallions Kala Shikari and the top-class miler, Young Generation. Although the stud buildings are still *in situ*, Wyld Court has not been used as a thoroughbred stud since Watkins's departure.

Another stud no longer used as such is the Head's Farm establishment at Chaddleworth. Owned by Tom Egerton, a Jockey Club member, the stud produced over the years from only a small band of mares some decent racehorses. Final Chord, Curtains, and Town and Country, sold to the then Lord Porchester during his racing career, all carried the Egerton colours with distinction. In the eighties, when Tom Egerton cut down his breeding interests, the stud was run as a boarding and livery establishment under the management of Bob McCreery. Now Charles Egerton, Tom Egerton's son, uses the old stud yard as a training stable. Taking out a licence for the 1991 season, Egerton trained a winner with his first ever runner, the steeplechaser Torrent Bay.

The Uplands stud at Compton also ceased to operate in the eighties. Built by Mrs Lusty in 1972, the stud was home for the good Lusty-owned sprinter, Native Bazaar, who was himself bred at Uplands. The stud was then bought by George Ward. David Arbuthnot trained from the old stud yard for a period before moving his string into stables in the village of Compton. Since then Uplands has ceased to operate as a stud.

Further back in time the Lodge Park Stud at Lambourn was a breeding establishment of note towards the end of the nineteenth century. Blankney, a son of Hermit, Henry Chaplin's Derby winner, stood at Lodge Park in the 1890s. Blankney was owned by Sir John Thursby, who patronized the Lamborne Place yard of James Humphreys at the time. Solly Joel built a stud at his home, Maiden Erlegh, near Reading. In the early years of the twentieth century, Joel had a racemare named Doris. When she broke down in training, he decided to sell her, believing she would have no value as a broodmare. Solly Joel's brother, J.B. Joel, told him he should not sell her as she had won races and was also named after one of his daughters. Solly Joel retorted that if his brother thought so well of the mare, he could have her. It was a remark S.B. Joel lived to regret: Doris became the dam of his brother's Derby winner of 1911 Sunstar, as well as the 1914 dual fillies' Classic winner, Princess Dorrie. Although Solly Joel did not enjoy as much success on the turf as his brother, he owned the 1915 triple crown winner, Pommern. Pommern was trained at Newmarket by Charles Peck, who handled S.B. Joel's string for many years.

The famous Whatcombe racing stables were the home of the great stallion Blandford for the last two years of his life. Bought as a yearling at Newmarket's December Sales by Dick Dawson for only 750 gns, Blandford was sent into training at Whatcombe, the property of Dawson and his brother, S.C. Dawson. Blandford proved to be a difficult horse to train, being heavy-topped and the possessor of a terrible pair of forelegs. He only ran four times in his racing career, winning three races including the Princess of Wales's Stakes at Newmarket. Shortly after his Newmarket victory he sustained a tendon injury, which necessitated his retirement. Dick Dawson, who had always believed that Blandford would have won a Derby if had been a sounder horse, decided to stand Blandford himself. He was dispatched across the Irish Sea to stand at the Dawson's family stud at Clogran near Dublin. Blandford became one of the greatest stallions of the twentieth century, siring four Derby winners, Trigo, Blenheim (both trained at Whatcombe by Dawson), Bahram and Mahmoud.

In 1933 the Dawson brothers were forced to move Blandford from Ireland to England to avoid a punitive bloodstock tax imposed by the British government. Blandford took up residence at Whatcombe. Within two years the great stallion was dead and was buried at Whatcombe. His grave, near the famous stables, is still visible to this day.

Perhaps the most important Berkshire stud of all was one which ceased to operate over 200 years ago. Cranbourne Lodge in Windsor Forest was where the Duke of Cumberland bred two colts destined to shape the history of the turf. Eclipse and Herod will be remembered as long as thoroughbreds are raced: their contribution to the breed has been discussed in the first chapter of this book. The important place in turf history which they occupy, as forefathers of the modern breed of racehorse, can never be overestimated.

The Arabs by sheer weight of money have assembled on their studs the most aristocratic of bloodlines. The British breeder consequently now finds it hard to compete against the Arab dominance on the racecourse. Many breeders have given up the unequal struggle, feeling they cannot compete with the talent which Middle-Eastern interests have assembled. In the boom years of the early eighties, commercial studs at the top end of the market made money: the Arabs were prepared to pay vastly inflated prices to buy young stock and mares of the great British bloodlines. The enormous bloodstock prices gained at the time created a false impression of the health of the breeding industry. Basically, those operating in the middle or lower ends of the market were losing money as a result of high stallion fees and production costs. When the recession arrived in the last years of the Thatcher era, studs at the top end of the market began to lose money as bloodstock prices plummeted. Their colleagues lower down the market fared worse than ever. Not only did they still continue to lose in the sale ring but their principal assets, their mares and their properties, devalued to a dangerously low level. This is the state of the breeding industry at the moment. Not only has it had to ride a depressed bloodstock market, it has also had to compete on unequal terms with its Irish and French neighbours. The disparity which exists between Great Britain's high VAT rate of 17.5 per cent and the far lower rates of France and Ireland, has made many breeders and owners prefer to buy, sell, train or keep their mares across the water. A rapid end to the recession and a change in the VAT laws are required by the breeding industry in Britain. Many British studs will be unable to cope with the current economic situation for much longer.

12
THE FUTURE OF BERKSHIRE RACING

What does the future hold for Berkshire's racing industry? The current recession in this country has brought havoc to the business world. Racing is no exception. The racehorse is an expensive toy to keep: with training fees and racing expenses likely to cost a minimum of £14,000 a year, without the original purchase price, and statistically little chance of recouping the investment, the racehorse is likely to be the owner's most expensive hobby. When times are hard, the hobbies and the luxuries are the first items to go. The British owner has become a scarcer commodity, increasingly unable to afford the most expensive luxury. The Lloyds débâcle and the present depressed condition of the property market are likely to make the British owner even scarcer.

A glance down any major flat race stable's list of owners will reveal a huge preponderance of foreign, particularly Middle Eastern, clients. These are the major owners of the modern day. The British owner-breeders of the past, the Lord Roseberys, Derbys and Astors have become a fast declining breed. Without Arab sponsorship, it is becoming increasingly difficult for trainers to compete at the highest level of flat racing. Paul Cole, the trainer of the 1991 Derby winner Generous, is certain that, if he did not have the support of the Saudi Prince Fahd Salman, Generous's owner, he would never have been able to attain his present position, let alone finance the purchase of Whatcombe. Trainers without Arab sponsorship and with declining British patronage, are finding it increasingly hard to stay in business. With the Arabs at the present competing in the jumping game in only a small way, the jumping trainer tends to rely on the domestic owner to fill his stable. Many report a dearth of orders for new horses: almost all cite the recession as the culprit. A decline in horse numbers creates problems, as the overheads and running costs of a training establishment remain virtually the same whether the yard is full or not.

If the recession has depleted the ranks of owners, it has also been responsible for a massive devaluation of training properties. In the boom years of the eighties, training stables were rapidly appreciating assets. Now the opposite is true. The decreasing value of these properties and the fact that the majority would not attract a buyer, if put on the open market, have destroyed from the point of view of the lending banks the trainer's principal source of collateral, and consequently his or her ability to secure their borrowings. Declining incomes and increasing bad debts have made it nearly impossible to make training a profitable profession in the current economic climate.

Massive staff cuts, which other industries employ when facing financial difficulty, are not the answer for the trainer. Businesses where animals are involved are by their very nature labour intensive. Consequently a trainer's wage bill is, compared to businesses of corresponding turnover, relatively high. Stable staff's wages, although close to the foot of the national scale, have in recent times received large annual percentage increases. £165 per week is now the recommended minimum wage. Although married men with children have been forced to leave the industry unable to make ends meet, the stable lad's lot, relative to twenty years or so ago, is now far better. The side effect of these wage increases has been that trainers have had to raise fees considerably on virtually an annual basis. A vicious circle has been created. Many owners have been forced to leave racing unable to afford the sky-high fees, in the main brought about by the annual negotiated pay rises.

Large training fee increases have not been accompanied by increases in prize money. Although the Jockey Club persuaded a House of Commons Select Committee that the bookmakers should contribute an extra £10m. to the Levy on top of their offer of some £38m. for 1992, increased prize money, which the extra sum will fund, will be very small across the board. The average British race will still be worth far less than its French, Australian or American counterpart. In Britain it is possible to win four races with a single horse in one year and still be out of pocket. Conversely, one win on a metropolitan Paris track will enable the owner to cover his year's training fees. The low level of prize money on British racecourses has been a major factor in the decline in British ownership on the turf. Sponsorship has been far harder to secure as a result of the recession. The newly conceived Festival of Racing, held in September at Ascot, is currently without an overall sponsor: Brent Walker, the original underwriter, is now beleaguered by financial difficulty and has been forced to withdraw. Other courses report similar difficulties in raising race sponsorship: Ascot is not alone in this respect.

Racing's overall financial position is dangerous. Low prize money has made the Arabs move far more horses to race overseas to take advantage of more lucrative prizes. Britain's high VAT rate of 17.5 per cent makes training or buying horses here a more costly practice than in Ireland or France. The decentralized nature of British racing adds large transport costs to owners' bills. If the decrease in turnover currently reported by bookmakers as a consequence of the recession continues, the increased levy of 1992 is not guaranteed to be maintained. After all, the yearly payment which the bookmakers make to racing is only a percentage of the total take. On a national scale the future looks unpromising.

The industry in Berkshire is as affected by the national malaise as other areas are. The horse population is down, the villages of East Ilsley and Compton being prime examples. East Ilsley ten years ago was home to four thriving training yards. Now only two trainers are resident there. Nelson House, where Roddy Armytage trained, has been developed for housing. Kim Bailey's yard at Hill House still awaits a buyer nearly two years after his move to new quarters in Lambourn. The neighbouring village of Compton, a thriving training centre in the fifties and sixties, is now home to fewer than fifty horses and only two trainers, Peter Cundell and David Arbuthnot.

Lambourn is suffering in the same respect. Stan Mellor's old yard at Linkslade on the Wantage road out of Lambourn is empty. College House in the High Street, one of the village's oldest yards, has been developed for housing. Delamere Stables, where Dave Hanley and Ray Laing trained, has in the main been turned into flats. Many famous names are training depleted strings at the present time. Peter Walwyn, Charlie Brooks, David Murray-Smith and even Jenny Pitman are notable examples. Paul Cole's departure to Whatcombe saw a large number of horses leave the village. Rumours abound that many yards in the centre are unofficially for sale, but unlikely in the present climate to secure a buyer.

On the plus side, Barry Hills's return from Manton and Dick Hern's arrival from West Ilsley to his newly constructed yard at Kingwood enabled the village horse population to gain a much needed increase. Peter Walwyn's sale of the Seven Barrows establishment to Nick Henderson and his return to his original quarters at Windsor House was a mutually acceptable arrangement, which ensures the continued occupancy of the famous Seven Barrows yard. Henderson's jumping string, one of the largest in the country, will make ample use of the tremendous facilities Walwyn created during his years there. Paul Cole is now training his largest ever string at Whatcombe capitalizing on his Trainers' Championship year of 1991. Cole brought Berkshire an overseas Classic success in 1992, his filly Culture Vulture winning the French 1,000 Guineas. William Huntingdon, the Queen's trainer at West Ilsley, has assembled a large string in 1992 and is having a most successful year. A royal victory in Ascot's Hunt Cup and a second successive Gold Cup have been the highlights of Huntingdon's year.

Lambourn trainers are conscious of the need to keep the famous village in the public eye. A highly successful open day is run yearly on Good Friday, to enable the public to visit the stables and see the thoroughbreds in action on the downs. Huge crowds attended in 1992. The proceeds of the open day, which raised over £23,000 in 1991, go in the main to the Lambourn Racing Welfare Fund. The fund's main purpose is to tackle the shortage of rented accommodation for stable employees in the village. Much has been achieved. Already five starter homes in the centre of the village have been purchased. The Lambourn Trainers' Association, who administer the fund, are determined that many more houses will be available in the years to come. Further publicity for the village has also been generated, as permission has been granted recently for signs to be erected on roads nearby and on the neighbouring M4 motorway, to publicize the village as a horse racing centre. 'Lambourn, the valley of the racehorse' is the logo which the signs will carry. Tours are arranged by the Lambourn Trainers Federation to enable parties to visit stables in the area, and a publicity brochure has been composed. Tours are also run to the village of Compton to see the location where the television series *Trainer* is made.

The decline in horsepower of the majority of trainers has a knock-on effect to all businesses either on the periphery or directly associated with the racing industry. Jobs for stable staff are of course harder to find, with many yards suffering depleted strings. Blacksmiths, vets, saddlers and feed merchants suffer a fall in income if the racehorse population drops. Studs and livery yards suffer in the same way. Livery yards require training stables to burst at the seams: the overflow is their bread and butter. Commercial studs require a buoyant market to sell their produce well at the sales to cover substantial overheads, and a sound economic situation to attract new clients and increase their stock: neither is prevalent at the present time. All sections of the industry look forward to the end of the current recession. An upturn of the economic situation is needed desperately, sooner rather than later.

Historically the Berkshire racing industry has survived hard times. Two World Wars, the General Strike, and the recession of the seventies brought problems that the industry was able to surmount. Although the current recession will claim more victims, Middle Eastern money should help racing ride the storm. Arab interests have invested heavily in the county. Khaled Abdullah's Juddmonte stud at Wargrave, Hamdan al Maktoum's new training complex at Kingwood, Lambourn and Whatcombe rebuilt with Fahd Salman's funds are pertinent examples.

The racecourses of Berkshire are investing in the future. The new stand at Newbury, scheduled to open at the 1992 Hennessy meeting, will make Newbury as modern a course as anywhere in the land. The executive will seek to use the new facilities for conferences and functions on as many days as possible when the course is not racing. Income derived from these outside sources is an important feature of modern racecourse management. Ascot is constantly renovating and improving its facilities. Attendance figures for the 1992 Royal fixture satisfied the executive, considering the country's current economic plight. Windsor still attracts vast crowds to its summer evening meetings and sponsorship there has stood up surprisingly well. Berkshire's courses have weathered the recession better than some of the country's other tracks: the Scottish racecourses of Edinburgh and Ayr are examples of racecourses with considerable financial problems. The county's racecourses consequently look secure for the forseeable future.

The modern all-weather gallop, significantly improved since its invention, has reduced the need for excellent grass gallops. Martin Pipe has proved that the all-weather surface can produce a jumper as fit as any grass terrain. The Arundel trainer John Dunlop has produced many top-class flat winners trained almost exclusively on artificial surfaces. The Berkshire trainer, though, has remained faithful to the traditional method of galloping on grass. They prefer to combine the use of the grass and artificial surfaces, using the all-weathers when the ground is either too hard or too soft, or for routine condition work. It is not so much that Pipe and Dunlop prefer the all-weather to the grass, it is more that their grass gallops are not of sufficient quality to train their top-class charges on. The Berkshire trainer is lucky in this respect. The turf of his grass gallops is old, springy, and in the main untouched by the plough. Proven over the centuries to be the perfect surface on which to gallop the racehorse, the training grounds look certain to survive for the forseeable future. The current poor state of the agricultural industry would suggest that Berkshire's gallops are secure from the ravages of the farmer's plough. In the past some famous gallops have been lost to agriculture. Cumberland's racecourse on Prestall Down near East Ilsley was ploughed at the beginning of the nineteenth century. The great Lord Lyon gallop near Harwell research centre perished for the Second World War agricultural effort. Others, such as Angel Down on the Shefford Road out of Wantage, used by Charles Morton for many classic workouts, and a gallop which ran north across the valley from Seven Barrows towards the Ridgeway east of Kingstone Warren, have also vanished: victims of the boom years of farming. The constitution of the downs remains the same, though. They were there before the thoroughbred racehorse evolved, and are Berkshire's oldest monument. The great Berkshire-trained horses have all trodden the ancient downland turf. Whatever fate or fortune befalls Berkshire's racing industry in the uncertain future, it is the nearest thing to a racing certainty that the downs will still be there two hundred years from now.

The training stables and the many businesses which support them require a more stable economic state to ensure their viability. As in other walks of life, the strong will survive and the weak will fall. At the moment the product which trainers have to offer, is unattractive to the prospective owner, British or foreign: the return on the investment does not compare favourably with the expense incurred. Those owners wealthy enough not to worry are not unfortunately on every trainer's books. Until the product is improved, with the vast majority of winning horses covering their training costs, the industry will have its work cut out to attract new custom. As training fees are most unlikely to decrease, the only answer must be to increase the prize money substantially. The question is, where will the money come from? At the moment the answer is unclear. Berkshire racing must hope the Jockey Club and their associates on the newly constructed British Horse Racing Board have some ideas. If not, the racehorses which exercise upon the famous Berkshire Downs will further decrease in numbers. If it is true that history repeats itself, the racing industry will rise again like a phoenix, stronger than before. However, if the industry's finances suffer further decline, it will be all the harder to restore it to its former glory. The many employed in or on the periphery of Berkshire racing must fervently hope that recovery is near at hand. Unfortunately their destiny is not in their own hands.

INDEX